SOMETHING TO CONSIDER

A FRESH LOOK AT SOME COMMON CHRISTIAN VIEWS (THEY MAY SURPRISE YOU!)

David L. Leatherman

Something to Consider
by David L. Leatherman

Printed in the United States of America

ISBN 1-60034-525-5

www.xulonpress.com

TABLE OF CONTENTS

Acknowledgment vii

Preface.. ix

Chapter 1 - The Old Testament and the New Testament.......... 13

Chapter 2 - The Reason for Truth and Righteousness 37

Chapter 3 - Tithing and Giving 45

Chapter 4 - A Rationale for the Existence of Good and Evil ... 55

Chapter 5 - Blessings and Miracles 63

Chapter 6 - What Could Anger Jesus? 71

Chapter 7 - I Need Help 81

Chapter 8 - Acts of Forgiveness 91

Chapter 9 - If You Love Me 101

Chapter 10 - The Islamic Religion and Muslims – The Truth . 115

Chapter 11 - A Plea to Christians – Wake Up and Smell the Muslims 133

Chapter 12 - Miscellaneous Thoughts 141

Chapter 13 - Inspirations on God's Greatest Creation – YOU 149

ACKNOWLEDGMENTS

Studying God's Word to understand His knowledge and His wisdom has been a hobby of mine. Because of my curiosity and analytical mind, I would take various topics from the Bible and study them in great detail. After the study was completed, a report was written, outlining the results of the study. Many of these reports were then handed out to various people, including ministers. Their reactions were very positive. Probably the most positive supporter of all who have read the reports has been my wife, Dorinda. I never had the intention of publishing these reports in the form of a book. She continuously encouraged me to do so. She, however, actually went beyond encouragement and became my editor as well as critic. She also enjoys the study of God's Word and has written and published a Bible study entitled "Out of the Storm, Into a Safe Haven." This is a study of God's healing for sexual abuse. For all that she has done to enable me to publish this book, I want to give a special acknowledgment of thanks.

There have also been many others who have encouraged me to publish these works. This confirmed what my wife thought must be done. I want to acknowledge those people for their encouragement and support

I also want to acknowledge two of my former office associates, Brandee Cook and Judy Davis. Thank you Brandee and Judy for the time you gave in the initial typing of these subject reports which are now being put in book form.

One last acknowledgment goes to my friend, Sara Greer, and my wife's sister, Gloria Wolfe, who did a great job of helping Dorinda edit this manuscript as proofreaders.

PREFACE

Deer Hunting. What does deer hunting have to do with God, spirituality, God's wisdom and understanding God's righteousness? Well, nothing in itself, except that it allowed me to have some very special sacred and uninterrupted time to seek God's truth and His wisdom.

While working for a Fortune 500 company in 1971, I came to know Jesus Christ as my personal Savior. It was a radical, 180-degree conversion for me. As with a lot of new Christians, mostly those with the gift of evangelism, I felt like I wanted to go into the mission field. As I look back on my life, I feel like the Lord directed me away from the Fortune 500 Company, away from my birthplace of Ohio, and into the field of financial services here in Tupelo, Mississippi. Much to my surprise, this became my geographical mission field, rather than Africa or some other foreign country. Although I have had the privilege of going on many foreign mission trips, here is where my appointed place is. While here in Tupelo, the Lord has directed my paths in many ways by opening doors to opportunities I could not have imagined.

When I first came to Tupelo, I found that deer abounded and deer hunting was the sportsman's ideal. I vowed I would never be a deer hunter, even though I was an avid hunter of small game in Ohio. However, as fathers are known to do, my interest changed with my young son's desire to learn how to deer hunt. Because of that, I became a deer hunter myself. While deer hunting never became a passion of mine, it became a vehicle to the next phase of my life.

There is really nothing to do in a deer stand, so I used that time to ask God to reveal His truths that He wanted me to know. It is amazing what He has revealed to me in those quiet times. I have also read many, many books and meditated a lot on God's Word. I believe God revealed many of His truths to me because I have asked and have taken the time to listen. Many of these truths were not common to my knowledge, wisdom and understanding. In talking with many who have read these writings, it was the same with them. What a privilege and great experience it has been to feel the heart and nature of God. This book is all about sharing those truths. Hopefully, the information in this book will give you some new insight on your relationship with God and on what you can expect from God and what He expects from you.

There are two fundamental truths I have learned from this study. First, God created all things and we were born into his creation. We are forced to abide by, and are controlled by, the physical and emotional laws that were put into place at creation. These laws will not change even when we try to defy them. When we try to defy these laws, we become victims of these laws. When we abide by them, we become a benefactor of the laws of creation. Some of the laws are physical laws and are very easy to understand. For instance, the law of gravity. If you jump up, you will come down. There are other physical laws governing life energy that we have studied in physics that also act upon us. Because they are physical and tangible, they are easily understood and accepted. These laws are essential for our system to work.

Now, as for the non-physical laws that govern our lives, - Most of these laws deal with our sin nature and do have an absolute bearing on our joy, peace, contentment and self identity. These laws may not be as obvious, yet they are just as real. These laws deal with our person-to-person relationships and to our relationship with our Creator – God, our Holy Father. These laws were put into place so that all creation can live in harmony. God sent His Son to show us how to live in harmony. These fundamental laws were revealed in the life of Jesus and are recorded in the New Testament. When you study the life of Jesus, there are two fundamental principles which drive all of the rest. Jesus showed us how to give and forgive. These two principles, giving and forgiving, are the secrets that govern the method by which all of God's creation can live in harmony. If you violate the laws laid out by Jesus, you cannot find lasting joy, peace, contentment or self worth. As an example, fornication, adultery, stealing, lying, homosexuality, etc. will only lead to self destruction and disharmony with oneself, with other people and with God.

So, the first truth you should consider is that you are born into a system that will control you. You will not control it. Your goal should be this: How can I live within the system of the rules and laws? The rules and laws book that contain all of the answers is the Holy Bible which is the last truth given to man. If you study the life of Jesus, you will see that all of the rules were put into place to provide a way for man to live in harmony. The two laws fundamental to all of the rest is to know how to give and forgive. Jesus' life exemplified these two laws.

The second truth I have learned is this: Jesus came to represent His Father as an act of mercy on humanity. Jesus came to shed His blood for our sins. Jesus came also to show His people all of the truth that the Holy Father wants us to know so that all who make a claim to the Holy Father through Jesus the Christ will become His ambassadors. There is not a choice in this matter. We are His ambassadors. The world would not have as many of the problems it has today if the Body of Christ would do what they have been commissioned to do – be His ambassadors. The second truth, then, is that we are the ambassadors of Christ.

I hope you enjoy reading this as much as I have enjoyed working with my Father to prepare it.

CHAPTER 1 -

THE OLD TESTAMENT AND THE NEW TESTAMENT

INTRODUCTION

For years I have been nagged by a curiosity to know and understand the difference between the Old Testament and the New Testament as well as a reason why there is an Old Testament and a New Testament. In this writing, I may use the terms "testament", "covenant", and "agreement" interchangeably since they have the same relative meanings. This curiosity was prompted by reading the scriptures and the confusion generated by what appeared to be differences between the Old Testament and the New Testament. I had an uneasy feeling about the application of each Testament as it applies to our own lives in our own relationship and responsibility to God today.

There appears to be an entirely different relationship between God and man in each of these covenants. Some clergy and Bible teachers seemed to be using these two Testaments interchangeably in such a manner that what I was being told did not seem to mix well. One thing seemed to contradict another. One particular concern of mine was the promises given to the people of the Old Testament and the promises given to the people of the New Testament. How did these promises compare and contrast?

After completing this study, I came to a resolve and a clarity of how I understood the difference between the Old Testament and the New Testament. I would like to share this resolve with you. Please read this with the understanding that it is not the end of my quest, but rather the beginning. As God works with me, some of these conclusions or resolves may change. But, at this point, I feel comfortable with what I have learned.

I challenge the reader to do the same thing. See what you can discover and see what God reveals to you from a study similar to this. It is very important to know our relationship to God - our covenant with God.

WHY IS THERE A NEED FOR A COVENANT BETWEEN MAN AND GOD?

In the beginning, God spoke the world into existence. He then saw that it was incomplete, so He created man and woman. He gave them the ability to live in total harmony within His creation and with Him as long as they refrained from one act - eating the fruit from one tree in the garden - the tree of the knowledge of good and evil. By giving into temptation, Eve ate from that tree and committed the first sin, followed by Adam's sin of disobedience to God's command as he also ate the fruit. Their sin opened the door for the necessity of rules and laws. Now, after they ate of the fruit, they were no longer in harmony with God. That was the beginning of the need for rules and laws in order to regain harmony with God. As time went on, God communicated through individuals such as Abraham and Moses and through prophets such as Elijah and Isaiah.

Abraham and Elijah, as well as many others, were the liaisons between God and man and communicated God's desires for their lives. The strict rules came down during Moses' time. The prime example of the law and the rules was The Ten Commandments as we call them. Why did God have to put these Ten Commandments into place as well as the other laws and rules? It is because of this: The people could not live in harmony, so to protect the welfare of His creation and the individuals within His creation. He had to send down hard rules that man must follow. These sets of rules included disciplinary actions for disobeying these rules as well as blessings for obeying them. God's relationship with man, for the most part, was that of a transactional relationship. He required man to do certain things to be blessed and to be in His favor. Law governed most of what needed to be done. So, it became a duty-driven, transactional-driven relationship with God where God did not walk among them but dealt with them through liaisons called priests. Jesus came to change that relationship with God, as you will see.

While the first relationship between God and man through the old covenant was a duty and transactional driven relationship, the new covenant brought forth a "desire" relationship. God wanted man to desire him and He used Jesus Christ as the example of the method for that desire. If I could break down the New Testament into the simplest form that I could understand, it would be this: Jesus came that we might be saved and to share with man the nature of His Holy Father. That nature is to give and to forgive. As you will see in the scriptures to follow, God no longer requires us to live by the Law to be justified but to live by grace through Jesus Christ. The grace is desire-driven rather than duty-driven.

ARE WE CURRENTLY UNDER THE AUTHORITY OF THE OLD TESTAMENT AND THE NEW TESTAMENT, OR JUST THE OLD TESTAMENT, OR JUST THE NEW TESTAMENT?

Consider the following passage from Scripture:

Hebrews 8 vs. 6-10

> *"But the ministry Jesus has received is as superior to theirs* (the priests) *as the covenant of which he is mediator is superior to the old one, and it is founded on better promises. For if there had been nothing wrong with that first covenant, no place would have been sought for another. But God found fault with the people and said, 'the time is coming, declares the Lord, when I will make a new covenant with the house of Israel and with the house of Judah. It will not be like the covenant I made with their forefathers when I took them by the hand to lead them out of Egypt, because they did not remain faithful to my covenant, and I turned away from them, declares the Lord. This is the covenant I will make with the house of Israel after that time, declares the Lord. I will put my laws in their minds and write them on their hearts. I will be their God and they will be my people'."*

Romans 4 clearly discusses the same subject. I interpret this just as it is written. The old covenant between God and man did not work. It required that a new covenant be put in place. A new covenant means just what it says - it is new. The old one is not required. The new one is in place of the old one.

The next logical question which comes is this: How are we to view the Old Testament with regard to how God wants us to relate to Him? The answer that I came up with is very simplistic. The first covenant between God and man was duty-driven. And it was more or less works-driven. Before God would bless, He required some form of action. Because of this, it was perceived that man was justified by following the law.

But justification has never been through the law. Justification has always been by grace through faith. Read Hebrews 11. By studying the New Testament, you can see that a person cannot be justified by doing works. Justification comes only by grace, which is possible through Jesus Christ. We can be justified by what He did at the cross and by His grace.

ARE WORKS, THE LAW AND SACRAMENTS NECESSARY UNDER THE NEW COVENANT?

Consider the following passage from Scripture:

Colossians 2 vs.13-17

> *"When you were dead in your sins and in the uncircumcision of your sinful nature, God made you alive with Christ. He forgave us all our sins, having canceled the written code with its regulations, that was against us and that stood opposed to us; he took it away, nailing it to the cross. And having disarmed the powers and authorities, he made a public spectacle of them, triumphing over them by the cross. Therefore do not let anyone judge you by what you eat or drink, or with regard to a religious festival, a new Moon celebration or a Sabbath day. These are a shadow of the things that were to come; the reality, however, is found in Christ".*

This passage of scripture addresses the question of works, the law and sacraments. While sacraments are not required for a relationship with God, they can be good to help sanctify your relationship. However, if the sacraments become an entity or hope for justification (becoming right with God), they are misused. In other words, sacraments, works and the law are never to become a means to be justified before God.

They are not necessary in order to have a relationship with the Holy Father. Justification through works was nailed to the cross with Jesus Christ and grace through the shed blood at the cross became our only justification.

Consider this and take it into account: The only recorded times that Jesus was driven to anger by the Pharisees and Teachers of the Law was when they demonstrated hypocrisy in the keeping the letter of the Law.

Consider the following passage from Scripture:

Romans 3 vs. 20-24

> *"Therefore, no one will be declared righteous in his sight by observing the Law, rather through the Law we become conscious of sin. But now righteousness from God, apart from the Law, has been made known, to which the Law and the Prophets testify. This righteousness from God comes through faith in Jesus Christ to all that believe. There is no difference, for all have sinned and fall short of the glory of God, and are justified freely by his grace through the redemption that came by Christ Jesus". (Emphasis mine)*

In the beginning, there was only one rule to keep in order to live in harmony with God. Enjoy all fruit in the garden except one. Do not eat of the fruit of the Tree of Life. When the one command was violated, Satan, in effect, was turned loose to bring disharmony into God's creation. The Law then became necessary. It described how man could live in harmony with God and with man. It also set forth the parameters within which man could find protection. Violate the Law and man was outside of God's protection from Satan.

WHY DID THE CHIEF PRIESTS, THE PHARISEES, AND THE SADDUCEES HATE JESUS?

Consider the following passage from Scripture:

Luke 22 vs. 1-2

> *"Now the Feast of Unleavened Bread, called the Passover, was approaching, and the chief priests and the teachers of the law were looking for some way to get rid of Jesus for they were afraid of the people".*

There are many verses relating to this, but these particular verses clearly show that the religious leaders did not want Jesus to disrupt the system that was in force. They were benefactors of that system and Jesus was altering that system. The old laws were, in general terms, centered on the proposition that "it is all about me." The new rule under Jesus is that it is not about me, but about my calling. **Here is an axiom that seems to be little known in some areas of the Christian community: We were not created to serve ourselves but to seek to serve others.** Just as Jesus came not to be served, but to serve.

Consider this passage from Scripture:

Matthew 20 vs. 25-27

> *"Jesus called them together and said, 'You know that the rulers of the Gentiles lord it over them and their high officials exercise authority over them. Not so with you. Instead, whoever wants to become great among you must be your servant, and whoever wants to be first must be your slave - just as the Son of Man*

did not come to be served, but to serve, and to give his life as a ransom for many'."

Refer also to Luke 22 vs. 27 and John 15 vs.15. Jesus is our example of serving others. He served His Father and those He walked among here on earth. Today He serves us by interceding for us before the Father. So, once again, the purpose of our creation is to love and serve God and to serve others. The Old Testament was, more or less, centered around God serving His people and His people serving Him on a *duty* basis. The New Testament is centered on a *desire* relationship with God. God *desires* to have us know and love Him and He wants us to *desire* to love Him. He wants our service to Him prompted out of love and not duty.

WHAT WAS THE PURPOSE OF THE LAW?

Consider the following passage from Scripture:

I Timothy 1vs.8-11

"We know that the law is good if one uses it properly. We also know that law is made not for the righteous, but for lawbreakers and rebels, the ungodly and sinful, the unholy and irreligious; for those who kill their fathers or mothers, for murderers, for adulterers and perverts, for slave traders and liars and perjurers - and for whatever else is contrary to the sound doctrine that conforms to the glorious gospel of the blessed God..."

The law was originally given to be a tutor (guardian) of conduct until the fulfillment of the law came through Jesus Christ.

Consider the following passage from Scripture:

Galatians 3 vs. 22-25

> *"For if a law had been given that could impart life, then righteousness would certainly have come by the law. But the Scripture declares that the whole world is a prisoner of sin, so that what was promised, being given through faith in Jesus Christ, might be given to those who believe. Before this faith came, we were held prisoners by the law, locked up until faith should be revealed. So, the law was put in charge as a tutor to lead us to Christ, that we might be justified by faith. (Emphasis mine.) Now that faith has come, we are no longer under the supervision of the law".*

The law was set in place so that man would not take advantage of another man and so that man could live in harmony with God's creation. God created the whole universe. He created the system of the physical laws. He created every part of our emotional and psychological behavior. His physical and spiritual laws, which were created in the beginning, have never changed. The things that will make man happy and sad are the same today as they were at creation. Man was born into this system. He cannot act upon the system. The system will simply act upon him. God laid down some principles so that man could live in harmony with one another and with his environment. This method of living in harmony is now within us because of Jesus and is directed by the Holy Spirit. Our guide reference is the Holy Scriptures.

WHO WAS THE MEDIATOR BETWEEN THE OLD COVENANT AND THE NEW COVENANT?

Consider the following passage from Scripture:

Hebrews 9 vs. 11-15

> *"When Christ came as high priest of the good things that are already here, he went through the greater and more perfect tabernacle that is not man-made, that is to say, not a part of this creation. He did not enter by means of the blood of goats and calves, but he entered the Most Holy Place once for all by his own blood, having retained eternal redemption. How much more, then, will the blood of Christ, who through the eternal Spirit offered himself unblemished to God, cleanse our consciences from acts that lead to death so that we may serve the living God! For this reason, Christ is the mediator of a new covenant, that those who are called may receive the promised eternal inheritance - now that he has died as a ransom to set them free from the sins committed under the first covenant".*

Scripture is clear that Jesus is the mediator of the new covenant, which secures our eternal inheritance and frees us from the law of the first covenant. Note: If we live by the law, then we are justified by the law. If we live by grace, then we are justified by grace. Through Jesus Christ we are released by grace from the law and are covered and protected by His grace. This covering and protection is sealed by the Holy Spirit at the moment we believe - at our salvation (Ephesians 1:13-14). That protection came with a price. The price was the cross and the resurrection.

DID JESUS COME TO REPLACE THE LAW OR TO ABOLISH THE LAW? OR DID JESUS COME TO FULFILL THE LAW?

Consider the following passage from Scripture:

Matthew 5 vs. 17-20 - Jesus speaking

> *"Do not think that I have come to abolish the Law or the Prophets. I have not come to abolish them but to fulfill them. I tell you the truth, until heaven and earth disappear, not the smallest letter, not the least stroke of a pen, will by any means disappear from the Law until everything is accomplished. Anyone who breaks one of the least of these commandments and teaches others to do the same will be called least in the kingdom of heaven, but whoever practices and teaches these commands will be called great in the kingdom of heaven. For I tell you that unless your righteousness surpasses that of the Pharisees and the teachers of the law, you will certainly not enter the kingdom of heaven".*

This passage can be a very delicate situation with me. In some sense, it seems to be a contrast to other things Jesus said. But, if you look at it carefully, there isn't necessarily a contrast. The question that comes, in my mind at least, is this: What is Jesus referring to when He refers to the law? Is He referring to the Mosaic Law, the Leviticus Law, or the original law at the time of Adam and Eve? There is a difference. The original law had to do with the manner in which man was made right with God. I believe Jesus was referring to that original law. Hebrews 9 makes clear what the original law was referring to.

Consider the following passage from Scripture:

Hebrews 9 vs. 16-22

> *"In the case of a will, it is necessary to prove the death of the one who made it, because a will is in force only when somebody has died; it never takes effect while the one who made it is living. This is why even the first covenant was not put into effect without blood. When Moses had proclaimed every commandment of the law to all the people, he took the blood of calves, together with water, scarlet wool and branches of hyssop and sprinkled the scroll and all the people. He said, "This is the blood of the covenant, which God has commanded you to keep." In the same way, he sprinkled with the blood both the tabernacle and everything used in its ceremonies. In fact, the law requires that nearly everything be cleansed with blood and without the shedding of blood there is no forgiveness." (Emphasis mine.)*

When Jesus said He came to fulfill the law, He could have been referring to the original law. All sin is redeemed only by a blood offering. Jesus was that offering for all past, present, and future sins. He therefore fulfilled the law. I take that to mean that Jesus is referring to those who choose to live under the Mosaic Law are responsible to the Mosaic Law. He did not come to change them who chose to believe in the Mosaic Law. However, there is enough scripture that leads me to believe that He did come to change the law for those who choose to not believe in the Mosaic Law, but to believe that He came to redeem us from the Law.

Those born in the dispensation of the Old Testament were under the laws of the Old Testament and still will be judged by those laws. Those who choose to live under the laws of the New Covenant will be judged by those laws. Here is the catch 22. To live and find justification under the Old Covenant was almost completely futile as it says in the scriptures. The only justification in the Old Testament that I can find came by faith. Abraham was saved by his faith, not by living up to the Law. This may be difficult to understand, however, I do feel as though I have an understanding of which Law Jesus came to fulfill. And this Law He came to respect and let stand.

WHEN DID THE NEW COVENANT BEGIN?

In my studies, I found this to be a very interesting question. My first inclination was to believe that the new covenant began at the death of Jesus Christ - until I was led to a scripture by a brother in Christ in Luke 16 vs. 16-17.

> *"The Law and the Prophets were proclaimed until John. Since that time, the good news of the kingdom of God is being preached and everyone is forcing his way into it. "It is easier for heaven and earth to disappear than for the least stroke of a pen to drop out of the Law."*

The way I read this, it is clear that the new covenant began with John the Baptist. Isn't that interesting? One of the main reasons that it is so interesting to me is the incident of the thief on the cross. How could he have been justified by grace if he died before Jesus Christ died and was under the Law? Since the new law began with John the Baptist, he was covered by the grace of Jesus Christ. Once again, that is extremely interesting to me.

Now that Jesus has come and brought the new covenant, we are the ministers of that covenant.

Consider the following passage from Scripture:

Hebrews 8 vs. 10-13

> *"This is the covenant I will make with the house of Israel after that time, declares the Lord. I will put my laws in their minds and write them on their hearts. I will be their God and they will be my people. No longer will a man teach his neighbor or a man his brother, saying "Know the Lord," because they will all know me from the least of them to the greatest. For I will forgive their wickedness and will remember their sins no more. By calling this covenant 'new', he has made the first one obsolete and what is obsolete and aging will soon disappear."*

The promise of a new covenant was given to the prophet Jeremiah. It is recorded in Jeremiah 31 and 32. Hebrews 8 vs. 10-13 is a direct quote of Jeremiah 31:33-34. Also in the book of Jeremiah, God records more of the new covenant He will bring forth through Jesus.

Consider the following passage from Scripture: Jeremiah 32 vs. 36

> *"They will be my people and I will be their God. I will give them singleness of heart and action, so that they will always fear me for their own good and the good of their children after them. I will make an everlasting covenant with them. I will never stop doing good to them and I will inspire them to fear me so that they will never turn away from me."*

This scripture gives us the assurance that as part of the new covenant, we have eternal security. God makes provision for that and then seals it with the Holy Spirit at the moment of conversion.

Consider the following passage from Scripture:

II Corinthians 3 vs. 4-9

> *"Such confidence as this is ours through Christ before God. Not that we are competent in ourselves to claim anything for ourselves, but our competence comes from God. He has made us competent as ministers of a new covenant - not of the letter but of the Spirit; for the letter kills, but the Spirit gives life. Now if the ministry that brought death, which was engraved in letters on stone, came with glory, so that the Israelites could not look readily at the face of Moses because of its glory, fading though it was, will not the ministry of the Spirit be even more glorious? If the ministry that condemns men is glorious, how much more glorious is the ministry that brings righteousness?"*

It is clear that God has made His chosen people ambassadors and ministers of the new agreement. It appears as though we are freed from the Mosaic Law as pointed out in II Corinthians 3 vs. 7 where it says in the NIV Bible "*if the ministry that brought death, which was engraved in letters on stone, which is referring to the Ten Commandments, came with glory so that the Israelites could not look readily at the face of Moses because of its glory, fading though it was, will not the ministry of the Spirit be even more glorious?*" There is an implication here that we are freed from the Ten Commandments laid out in the Mosaic Law. I would not venture to say that's an absolute. It appears to be that way. The other thing that is there in both of these scriptures is that the Lord has laid upon our hearts the laws He wants us to have and if we would yield to Him, these laws are no longer from the outside in but rather, from the inside out. And, it follows that our conduct would be from the inside out and no longer from the outside in. This brings me back to another of the same premise that I have been coming to for some time. The first covenant was duty driven and transactional driven. Jesus brought a new covenant of desire and put within us the reasons why we should desire Him. If we do not desire Him, it is not because it is not within us or the knowledge of the reason why it should be within us, because of what He did on the cross. What Jesus did on the cross should be the motivating force for us to desire to love and serve Him.

HOW DOES THE NEW AGREEMENT SAVE US AND FREE US?

Consider the following passage from Scripture:

Romans 4 vs. 13-15

> *"It was not through law that Abraham and his offspring received the promise that he would be heir of the world, but through the righteousness that comes by faith. For if those who live by law are heirs, faith has no value and the promise is worthless because law brings wrath. And where there is no law, there is no transgression."*

Romans 4 is an extremely interesting chapter with regard to the Law. It would serve you well to read the entire chapter in great detail. Verses 13, 14, and 15 clearly state that the Old Testament laws condemned us. The New Testament laws save us by grace through faith. When it says that the Old Testament laws condemned us, I would understand that to mean that it was impossible to be justified by works of the Law.

WHY IS THE NEW AGREEMENT (THE NEW TESTAMENT) REAL TO SOME AND NOT REAL TO OTHERS?

Consider the following passage from Scripture:

II Corinthians 3 vs. 14-16

> *"But their minds were made dull, for to this day the same veil remains when the old covenant is read. It has not been removed because only in Christ is it taken away. Even to this day when Moses is read, a veil covers their hearts. But whenever anyone turns to the Lord, the veil is taken away."*

These verses fully state that the truth about the new agreement is kept from them because they do not believe in Jesus Christ. This in itself is extremely interesting. If you do not believe in Jesus Christ, then you are under the Law and justified by the Law. It is a futile attempt to be justified by Law. So says the scripture. Only Jesus Christ reveals the new agreement - the new Covenant - that our justification comes by grace through faith in Jesus Christ.

DID GOD HAVE A RIGHT TO CHANGE FROM ONE COVENANT TO ANOTHER COVENANT? AND IS IT JUSTIFIED FOR SOME TO BELIEVE IN JESUS CHRIST AND OTHERS NOT TO BELIEVE IN JESUS CHRIST?

Consider the following statements taken from the subject matter of Romans 9:

Romans 9 gives a clear delineation of what our rights are and what God's rights are. God can choose to do what He wants to do. It clearly states in the scriptures that God gave His first chosen people every opportunity time after time after time to live within the agreement that He set up with them. And time after time after time they chose not to. So, God was justified and had the right to change His agreement between Himself and His people. Because of this change in the agreement, He allowed the Gentiles to be grafted into the Vine of the first chosen as it says in Romans 9. I don't personally understand all of this and probably never will. The interesting question again is, if the first chosen had lived by the rules, would we as Gentiles, have ever had a chance to be grafted into the vine of the first chosen? That's kind of an interesting and scary thought. Read Romans 9 carefully to find out what God's rights are and what our rights are.

A WARNING TO CHRISTIANS FROM THE OLD COVENANT'S HISTORY AND ISRAEL'S HISTORY

The first Covenant was a perfect Covenant. People could have lived in total harmony with each other and all of creation if the people had lived in the discipline of the first contract. They did not live within the Covenant/contract and were therefore punished. This punishment became an object lesson. A new Covenant, between man and God, was called the new testament. This new Covenant is also being violated. The verdict is still out on how God will deal with this violation and disobedience. Paul explains this in his letter to the Corinthians.

Consider 1 Corinthians 10 v 1-13

WARNINGS FROM ISREAL'S HISTORY - UNDER THE OLD COVENANT

"For I do not want you to be ignorant of the fact, brothers, that our forefathers were all under the cloud and that they all passed through the sea. They were all baptized into Moses in the cloud and in the sea. They all ate the same spiritual food and drank the same spiritual drink; for they drank from the spiritual rock that accompanied them, and that rock was Christ. Nevertheless, God was not pleased with most of them; their bodies were scattered over the desert.

"Now these things occurred as examples, to keep us from setting our hearts on evil things as they did. Do not be idolaters, as some of them were; as it is written: "The people sat down to eat and drink and got up to indulge in pagan revelry." We should not commit sexual immorality, as some of them did - and in one day twenty-three thousand of them died. We should not test the Lord, as some of them did - and were killed by snakes. And do not grumble, as some of them did - and were killed by the destroying angel. (Emphasis mine.)

"These things happened to them as examples and were written down as warnings for us, on whom the fulfillment of the ages has come. So, if you think you are standing firm, be careful that you don't fall! No temptation has seized you except what is common to man. And God is faithful; he will not let you be tempted beyond what you can bear. But when you are tempted, he will also provide a way out so that you can stand up under it." (Emphasis mine.)

WHAT IS THE PURPOSE OF THE OLD COVENANT AND THE LAW WITHIN THAT COVENANT? HOW DOES THE OLD COVENANT PREPARE MAN FOR THE PROMISES IN THE NEW COVENANT?

It is obvious after reading I Corinthians 10 v 1-13 (the previous paragraph) and Galatians 3 vs. 15-25 and 3 vs. 26-28, plus 4 vs. 1-7, that the Old Testament is an historical record of how God dealt with man's obedience and disobedience to the law under the Old Covenant. We are now under a New Covenant and our obedience to the New Covenant is just as important to God as it was for man under the Old Covenant. The Old Covenant becomes an object lesson for obedience. IMPORTANT: The Old Testament was all about God's relationship to man. The New Testament is all about man's relationship to God. Man's role and many of the promises associated with that role have changed from the Old Covenant to the New Covenant. In Galatians 3 vs. 15-25 and 3 vs. 26-29, plus 4 vs. 1-7. Paul discusses roles and promises and the law and how Jesus came to edify the original promise of the seed of Abraham.

Consider Galatians Chapter 3 vs. 15-25 – The Law and the Promise

> *"Brothers, let me take an example from everyday life. Just as no one can set aside or add to a human covenant that has been duly established, so this is in this case. The promises were spoken to Abraham and to his seed. The Scripture does not say 'and to seeds' meaning many people, but 'and to your seed' meaning one person, who is Christ. What I mean is this: The law, introduced 430 years later, does not set aside the covenant previously established by God and thus do away with the promise. For if the inheritance*

depends on the law, then it no longer depends on a promise; but God in his grace gave it to Abraham through a promise.

What, then, was the purpose of the law? It was added because of transgressions until the Seed to whom the promise referred had come. The law was put into effect through angels by a mediator. A mediator, however, does not represent just one party; but God is one.

Is the law, therefore, opposed to the promises of God? Absolutely not! For if a law had been given that could impart life, then righteousness would certainly have come by the law. But the Scripture declares that the whole world is a prisoner of sin, so that what was promised, being given through faith in Jesus Christ, might be given to those who believe.

Before this faith came, we were held prisoners by the law, locked up until faith should be revealed. So the law was put in charge to lead us to Christ that we might be justified by faith. Now that faith has come, we are no longer under the supervision of the law"

Consider Galatians chapter 3 vs. 26-29, and 4 vs. 1-7 – Sons of God

"You are all sons of God through faith in Christ Jesus, for all of you who were baptized into Christ have clothed yourselves with Christ. There is neither Jew nor Greek, slave nor free, male or female, for you are all one in Christ Jesus. If you belong to Christ, then you are Abraham's seed, and heirs according to the promise.

What I am saying is that as long as the heir is a child, he is no different from a slave, although he owns the whole estate. He is subject to guardians and trustees until the time set by his father. So also, when we were children, we were in slavery under the basic principles of the world. But when the time had fully come, God sent his Son, born of a woman, born under law, to redeem those under law, that we might receive the full rights of sons. Because you are sons, God sent the Spirit of his Son into our hearts, the Spirit who calls out, "Abba, Father." So you are no longer a slave, but a son; and since you are a son, God has made you also an heir"

CONCLUSION

The truth and a rationale for truth are written on the pages to follow. It is a driving force. There is a surprising amount of Scripture committed to an explanation of and a justification of the Old and New Testaments. The entire Old Testament pointed to Jesus Christ, who was to be the mediator of the new covenant. Some portions of Scripture are clearer than others. Read the book of Jeremiah, which gives a clear revelation of the new covenant that was to come. The New Testament is also very clear on this subject. Read Romans 1-15, I Corinthians 6-15, Galatians 2-6, and the whole book of Hebrews. The other books of the Bible have small portions related to the two covenants.

The book of Romans gives the justification of the Gentiles. The first 15 chapters of the book of Romans deal with the Roman Jews converted to Christianity. Because of their status of being the elect, these converted Jews resented the fact that an invitation was given to the Gentiles to be grafted into the vine of the first chosen into the brotherhood of Christ. Paul goes through an exhaustive delineation of why the Gentiles were grafted into the vine of the first chosen. He goes through a delineation of the elect and how under the first covenant, the first chosen, the elect, did not live up to the first covenant agreement. The first covenant did not work. The first chosen did not maintain what was necessary to sustain the first covenant agreement which created a need for a new agreement. The new agreement or covenant opened the door to the Gentiles with Jesus, the Christ, as the mediator.

CHAPTER 2 -

THE REASON FOR TRUTH & RIGHTEOUSNESS

THE REASON FOR TRUTH

The truth of God's creation is not a concern under my control. I am simply subject to that truth. What matters to me is the pursuit of that truth. In the text of theology, what is true is always true and what is false is always false. Truth cannot change. Prior to the coming of Jesus, the truth of all creation was given by God to certain men who were responsible for disseminating that truth. They were most commonly referred to as prophets. The Scriptures tell us in Hebrews that Jesus came to fulfill the law and to begin a new dispensation and reveal the last and complete truth to be given to man. When He came, we were released from all the Leviticus laws, rituals, sacrifices, and services of the previous dispensation. We were given a new covenant (agreement between God and His people). Under the old covenant, man, in general, could not look upon God or even be in the presence of God. God chose only a few to intercede on man's behalf and even then only at specified times. Jesus came to bring the new covenant whereby all men at any time can go directly to God through

Him. The Bible says there is only one mediator now between God and man - Jesus (I Timothy 2:5). The priesthood is no longer needed or wanted (Hebrews 9:18-19). Another person such as a priest or pastor acting as a mediator is not only not needed any longer, but is actually not wanted in light of the dispensation to come. The Scripture says at the death of Jesus, the veil between man and the presence of God in the Holy of Holies (which only a priest could enter and only once a year) was ripped from top to bottom. This is all very important because now Jesus is the ONLY mediator between God and man. NOW JESUS AND HIS TRUTH (the Scriptures) will be the source of all truth.

In the last dispensation, (the next dispensation to come), man and/or an organization will be part of the great deception. The great deception will ultimately try to reenact the previous dispensation that, among other things, separated man from God through the priesthood or prophets. That is what Jesus came and died to release us from. Basically, the great deception will try to once again elevate man or an entity such as a church as God. If that can be done, then man can choose to live by the standard he devises. Time and again we are rebuked by Scripture to test all things to the new covenant. We are to test all human teachers, and yes, even the clergy. Any lion can wear the cloak of a sheep and for awhile appear to be a sheep. Therefore, truth and the basis of truth is very important. Jesus spoke in John 8:32 that the truth will set you free. This quote is misused by much of the Christian community as well as the secular community. Study the text of this verse and you will see its correct meaning. The truth that the secular world has to offer does not set you free, but rather makes you captive to it and you are enslaved by it. On the other hand, the truth of the Holy Father through Jesus Christ, who brought the indwelling of the Holy Spirit, does not enslave you, but rather, really sets you free. Why do I seek truth? Because it sets me free and I want to be free.

My final resolve is this: If Jesus is <u>not</u> who He said He was, then I do not have time for Him. If He <u>is</u> who He said He was, I <u>cannot</u> live apart from Him.

One of my favorite verses in the Old Testament is Proverbs 2 vs. 1-6.

> *"My son, if you receive my words, and treasure my command within you,*
> *So that you incline your ear to wisdom*
> *And apply your heart to understanding;*
> *Yes, if you cry out for discernment*
> *And lift up your voice for understanding;*
> *If you seek her as silver,*
> *And search for her as for hidden treasures;*
> *Then you will understand the fear of the Lord*
> *And find the knowledge of God;*
> *For the Lord gives wisdom;*
> *From His mouth come knowledge and understanding".*

RIGHTEOUSNESS

Our Holy Father desires that we, His elect, would <u>desire</u> righteousness. To be sure it is understood which form of righteousness I am referring to, I will define it. Righteousness - a process of attaining and conforming to a standard that embraces what is right, just, and virtuous and morals according to the standard set forth by our heavenly Father and characterized by the life of Jesus Christ. Righteousness expresses itself in the form of what Jesus came to show us. Jesus showed us how to give and forgive. The Old Testament was a lot about receiving and the New Testament is all about giving.

Question: Why is righteousness important to the new covenant? God sent Jesus to show how man could live in total harmony with Himself and with other parts of His creation. If this could be done, then God could conquer sin and Satan through His servant man. In order to do this, however, man's mindset and ambitions would have to be in harmony with God's desires. This would require that man's desires would be to give and to forgive as Jesus taught. Righteousness, which is God's standard, would become the mode of living and therefore the method to that end. A love for God, mankind and for His creation would be the result. This brings us back to one of God's primary objectives - to conquer sin and create harmony in His creation. The method of conquering changed after the old covenant. The old covenant method of conquering was with might and wars. The new covenant method is love and peace. The harmony with God and with His creation is achieved through righteousness and holiness. The means to the method of the new covenant is so pragmatic and simple. Here it is: THE ONLY WAY THAT MAN CAN LIVE IN HARMONY WITH GOD, WITH EACH OTHER AND WITH THE REST OF CREATION IS THROUGH WHAT JESUS TAUGHT US - TO GIVE AND FORGIVE. One of my favorite passages of Scripture can be a guide for this. Consider Philippians 2 vs.1-8 quoted from The Living Bible.

> *"Is there any such thing as Christians cheering each other up? Do you love me enough to want to help me? Does it mean anything to you that we are brothers in the Lord, sharing the same Spirit? Are your hearts tender and sympathetic at all? Then make me truly happy by loving each other and agreeing wholeheartedly with each other, working together with one heart and mind and purpose. Don't be selfish; don't live to make a good impression on others. Be humble, thinking of others as better then yourself. Don't just think about your own affairs, but be*

interested in others, too, and in what they are doing. Your attitude should be the kind that was shown to us by Jesus Christ, who, though He was God, did not demand and cling to His rights as God, but laid aside His mighty power and glory, taking the disguise of a slave and becoming like men. And He humbled Himself even further, going as far as actually to die a criminal's death on a cross."

Only through the knowledge of our Holy Father's desires through the example of Jesus Christ who dwells within us through the Holy Spirit can we know righteousness. As it says in the Scriptures, God put within us a sense of right and wrong but true righteousness was modeled by Jesus and is reflected in His Word. Jesus came to show us how to give. Why then, are there scriptural references to ask and you will receive? Is there a conflict? The answer is no. There is no conflict. Why? If you study the context of the passages on asking, you will see that in each case, the reason to ask from the Lord would be to enrich and enhance our relationship with the Father so that we would be made more righteous. Outlined in the closing paragraphs is a brief discussion of that subject.

John 14 vs. 14

"You may ask for anything in my name, and I will do it."

This Scripture is used out of context so often and it is very frightening. If you use this Scripture and let it stand on its own, then that would be a license to get anything you want. However, that's not the intent of what Jesus said. Throughout the Scripture, we are told that we are called according to a purpose and to His purpose. There is a presumption, even within the Christian community, that God created us so that He could serve us rather then the reality that God created us so that we can worship and serve Him. The context of the John 14:14 passage is this: Jesus is preparing His disciples for the fact that He will no longer be there with them. He is in the midst of revealing that He and the Holy Father are one. And He is preparing them for their mission as disciples. These disciples will go out into the mission field and serve according to their purposes. In the process of preparing His disciples, the Lord said, "Ask me for anything in my name and I will do it." The phrase "in my name" means that which is according to Christ's character and God's will. What Jesus is referring to is anything according to the disciples' mission, not for their personal gain. Do you see this is not a reference to self but rather a means to His mission? Immediately after He tells the disciples this, He prepares them for the Holy Spirit.

Jesus further expands upon this very same subject in chapter 15. Verse 7 says "*If you remain in Me and my words remain in you, ask whatever you wish and it will be unto you.*" Again, the whole context of asking and receiving is about our mission as disciples for the Lord. Read Chapter 15:1-17. You will find that it clearly delineates that truth.

Once again, if John 14 vs.14 is taken out of context, the presumption is that God created us so that He could serve us, which is not true at all, because God created us so that we could love and serve Him, and Jesus became the example for us.

There is a fine line between our own ambition and God's desires for us. Often times, preachers, as well as lay persons, will fractionalize the Scripture and will use selective passages to justify their preconceived ambitions and desires instead of using Scripture in the context of His text. God may allow man's ambition to succeed, but it doesn't mean that He desires it. In every instance in the New Testament, every reference to our asking for, and receiving, is in reference to a preparation for righteousness and holiness so that we might serve our Father as an ambassador for Him. The whole basis of blessing changed from the Old Covenant to the New Covenant. In the Old Covenant, most, if not all, blessings were transactional. If man did something, God would bless. In the New Covenant, we serve out of a desire, not as a duty. An example would be from the Old Testament command to honor your father and mother so that you will be blessed. The New Covenant sets forth the command to honor your father and mother because you love God and because you have already been blessed.

Matthew 7 vs. 7

> *"Ask and you will be given what you ask for."*

If this verse could stand on its own, then there would be no end to what we would ask for to serve our own vanity, ambitions, and desires. This verse is not intended to stand on its own. Check its context. Jesus is referring to holiness, sanctification and righteousness. The rest of the verse says, "Seek and you will find. *Knock and the door will be opened.*" To a Christian, this should mean - Ask, as a means to righteousness and holiness and it will be given to you.

CONCLUSION

The conclusion of this analysis is self-evident. If the conclusion is not self-evident, then I can say no more.

CHAPTER 3 -

TITHING AND GIVING

Tithing may not be a requirement of the new covenant. In fact, it may not be desired. This could appear to be a bodacious statement, but let's explore the rationale. Analyze the New Covenant and see what it says. There are references to tithing as given as a command in the Old Testament, but no edict to tithe in the New Testament. Actually, in this area of righteousness, it could be a curse. Wow! How can a statement like that be made? That statement can be made on the presumption that our Holy Father delights in *desire* more than *duty*. Tithing was a duty that was transactional to blessings. The New Testament speaks of a different reason for giving and a different way of giving back to the Lord. While tithing *can be* a model, it is no longer required as a duty, and it is certainly not a prerequisite to blessings, *necessarily*. Notice that I put a qualification on that last statement - not necessarily. Tithing was a commandment, law and duty under the old covenant. Under the new covenant, we are asked to give. Giving is a free-will response driven by desire. Giving then becomes offerings unto the Lord. Under the old covenant, 10% of the first fruits was required. The new covenant does not limit giving to 10% (more than, or less than) and extends beyond measure of the first fruits of our labor. The new covenant also requires a giving of yourself. The new covenant requires 100% of self. It is my opinion that our Lord is more pleased with a giving of self over the giving of the first fruits.

I believe the above statements can be supported by Scripture. The Scriptures governing giving under the new covenant and the conclusions concerning tithing/giving become self-evident.

HOW WAS THE TEN PERCENT STANDARD ESTABLISHED?

Hebrews 7 vs.1-2 (The Living Bible)

> *"This Melchizedek was king of the city of Salem and also a priest of the Most High God. When Abraham was returning home after winning a great battle against many kings, Melchizedek met him and blessed him. Then Abraham took a tenth of all he had won in battle and gave it to Melchizedek. Melchizedek's name means 'Justice,' for he is the King of Justice and he is also the King of Peace because of the name of the city, Salem, which means 'Peace'."*

Isn't it interesting that God established 10% as a just amount to give back to Him and used Melchizedek, whose name means "Justice?" Justice and righteousness are interchangeable in this passage of Scripture.

TITHES - INSTRUCTIONS FOR THE USE OF AND THE PURPOSE OF THE TITHE AS IT APPLIES TO THE FIRST COVENANT

Deuteronomy 14 vs. 22-29

"Be sure to set aside a tenth of all that your fields produce each year. Eat the tithe of your grain, new wine and oil, and the firstborn of your herds and flocks in the presence of the Lord your God at the place he will choose as a dwelling for his Name, so that you may learn to revere the Lord your God always. But if that place is too distant and you have been blessed by the Lord your God and cannot carry your tithe (because the place where the Lord will choose to put his Name is so far away), then exchange your tithe for silver, and take the silver with you and go to the place the Lord your God will choose. Use the silver to buy whatever you like: cattle, sheep, wine or other fermented drink, or anything you wish. Then you and your household shall eat there in the presence of the Lord your God and rejoice. And do not neglect the Levites living in your towns, for they have no allotment or inheritance of their own.

"At the end of every three years, bring all the tithes of that year's produce and store it in your towns, so that the Levites (who have no allotment or inheritance of their own) and the aliens, the fatherless and the widows who live in your towns may come and eat and be satisfied, and so that the Lord your God may bless you in all the work of your hands."

The scripture says (in verse 23) the tithe is used *"so that you may learn to revere the Lord God always"*.

The scriptures also say that the tithe would serve the Lord in this way — *"so that the Levites (who have no allotment or inheritance of their own) and the aliens, the fatherless and the widows who live in your towns may come and eat and be satisfied, and so that the Lord your God may bless you in all the work of your hands"*.

Isn't it wonderful that our Lord has a tremendous passion and love for the "*least of His people*". The Lord also showed that passion through Jesus. Jesus also had a passion for the "*least of His people*". Somehow, I wonder if Christianity in its form today has either dulled it's senses to or lost sight of the primary passion of our Lord and His Son, Jesus—- *"The least of His people"*. Jesus revealed his desire for His followers and the Church as he expressed it in Matthew 25: 14-30. *"When you have done this unto the least of these, you have done it unto to Me."*

JESUS CAME AS AN OFFERING

Hebrews 8 vs. 3-6

> *"For every high priest is appointed to offer both gifts and sacrifices. Therefore it is necessary that this One also has something to offer. For if He were on earth, He would not be a priest, since there are priests who offer the gifts according to the law; who serve the copy and shadow of the heavenly things as Moses was divinely instructed when he was about to make the tabernacle. For He said 'See that you make all things according to the pattern shown you on the mountain'. But no; He has obtained a more excellent ministry, inasmuch as He is also Mediator of a better covenant, which was established on better promises."*

Jesus came as an offering on our behalf, but not as prescribed by law (verse 4). He came superior to the old required law as a mediator to the new law which is founded on better promises.

WHAT IS THE STANDARD OF GIVING AS STATED IN THE NEW COVENANT?

Consider the following passages:

II Corinthians 9 vs. 5-7

> *"Therefore I thought it necessary to exhort the brethren to…prepare your generous gift beforehand…that it may be ready as a matter of generosity and not as a grudging obligation. But, this I say, 'He who sows sparingly will also reap sparingly, and he who sows bountifully will also reap bountifully.' So, let each one give as he purposes in his heart, not grudgingly or of necessity, for God loves a cheerful giver."*

A reason for giving is explained in II Corinthians 9 vs. 8-9

> *"And God is able to make all grace abound toward you, that you, always having all sufficiency in all things, may have an abundance for every good work. (My emphasis) As it is written:*
>
> *'He has dispersed abroad,*
> *He has given to the poor;*
> *His righteousness endures forever."*

And in II Corinthians 9 vs. 11, we find that any increase in wealth that we receive is for the purpose of giving.

"Now may He who supplies seed to the sower and bread for food supply and multiply the seed you have sown and increase the fruits of your righteousness while you are enriched in everything for all liberality which causes thanksgiving through us to God."

Based on these Scriptures, therefore, it does not sound like man is being coerced into ritually giving 10% out of duty. It sounds as if God wants you to desire to give what is purposed in your heart. For some that my be much more than 10% and for some, less than 10%. If the new covenant Scriptures do not require 10%, why should any man or the clergy require it?
I Corinthians 16 vs. 2 shows us a standard for our giving.

"On the first day of the week let each one of you lay something aside, storing up as he may prosper, that there be no collections when I come".

To give as you are prospered - that is not a measure, that is quantifiable.
II Corinthians 8 vs. 1-5

"Moreover, brethren, we make known to you the grace of God bestowed on the churches of Macedonia; that in a great trial of affliction, the abundance of them and their deep poverty abounded in the riches of their liberality. For I bear witness that according to their ability, yes, and beyond their ability, they were freely willing, imploring us with much urgency that we would receive the gift and the fellowship of the ministering to the saints. And not only as we had hoped, but they first gave themselves to the Lord and then to us by the will of God."

The church of Macedonia gave as much as they were able, but it pleased Paul most because they gave themselves first.

HOW DOES GOD FEEL ABOUT A PERSON WHO GIVES OUT OF DESIRE RATHER THAN OUT OF DUTY OR IN EXPECTATION OF A REWARD (BLESSING)?

Consider the following passage from Scripture:

Luke 21 vs. 1-4

> *"And He looked up and saw the rich putting their gifts into the treasury, and He saw also a certain poor widow putting in two mites. So He said, 'Truly I say to you that this poor widow has put in more than all, for all these out of their abundance have put in offerings for God, but she out of her poverty put in all the livelihood that she had.'*

Jesus did not appear to be impressed with the quantity of the gifts but rather the heart of the giver. While the others gave out of abundance, the widow gave out of desire. How did He react to the gift of the poor widow?

JESUS PUT A STIPULATION ON GIVING.

Consider the following passage from Scripture:

Matthew 5 vs. 23-24

> *"Therefore, if you bring your gift to the altar, and there remember that your brother has something against you, leave your gift there before the altar and*

go your way. First be reconciled to your brother and then come and offer your gift."

In a sense, Jesus really only wants kosher giving or offerings. He is a Holy God who does not need unholy offerings (money). It sounds as if He does not even *want* unholy money. It seems strange that we never hear this *condition* for giving preached from the pulpit.

GIVING VS. TRANSACTING

If I said I would give you a dollar if you polished my shoes, would that be giving or transacting? Of course, it would be transacting. That same principle is true of all aspects of giving. If you give with an expectation of a return, you have not *given* at all, but rather *transacted*. True giving has no expectation of a return. Question: If I tithed (gave 10%) with the idea and expectation that the money would improve the appearance or the comfort level of the church, did I really, really tithe? Tithing is supposed to be *giving*.

UNACCEPTABLE OFFERINGS: GIVING OR TITHING

Consider the following passages from Scripture. Notice in the passages that follow, that our Lord puts a stipulation on giving, tithing, or sacrificing. If it is done for the wrong reasons, or if it is done by an unholy person, then the Lord rebukes the gift. Under the terms of the new covenant, the Lord wants a gift given out of desire, rather than duty as illustrated in Acts 8 vs. 20-21.

Genesis 4 vs. 5

"The Lord looked with favor on Abel and his offering, but on Cain and his offering he did not look with favor."

Proverbs 15 vs. 8

"The Lord detests the sacrifice (the gifts/tithes) of the wicked, but the prayer of the upright pleases him."

Jeremiah 6 vs. 20

"What do I care about incense from Sheba or sweet calamus from a distant land? Your burnt offerings are not acceptable; your sacrifices do not please me."

Amos 5 vs. 22

"Even though you bring me burnt offerings and grain offerings, I will not accept them. Though you bring choice fellowship offerings, I will have no regard for them."

Isaiah 1 vs.11

"The multitude of your sacrifices (the gifts/tithes) what are they to me?, says the Lord. I have more than enough of burnt offering.".

Acts 8 vs. 20-21

"Peter answered, May your money perish with you, because you thought you could buy the gift of God

with money! You have no part or share in this ministry, because your heart is not right before God."

THE BIG QUESTION

Giving, tithing, offering, or whatever you choose to call it, should be an expression of love to the Lord. If it is an obligation, beware! The big question is <u>not</u> how much is given for the sake of the Lord, but how much is kept for the sake of self.

<u>CONCLUSION</u>

As I said in the opening paragraph, the conclusions are self-evident. I know what I have concluded. After this analysis, coupled with your own research, what have you concluded?

CHAPTER 4 -

RATIONALE FOR THE EXISTENCE OF GOOD AND EVIL

PREFACE

The paradox of good and evil coexisting in a loving God's creation was a concept that at one time was baffling to me. It was also a question frequently asked by others as I witnessed to them about God or as I participated in general discussions. Through much prayer in asking God for wisdom and His way, through reading authors such as C. S. Lewis, A. W. Tozier, Lee Strobel, and others and through reading God's Word, I came to the following as an understanding of this subject. Hopefully, this understanding will have as much value to others as it has to me.

THE COEXISTENCE OF GOOD AND EVIL

If God is truly God and totally just and in control of His creation - how can both good and evil exist? The answer comes down to free will. We have the free will of choice. If God did not set a standard for what is good and what is evil, then there would be no choice. If only good existed, then our choice would have been made for us. If we were told we had no choices and we had one and only one direction we could go - then that would probably not in itself be good. Good and evil are relative and related. Good can not exist without the option of evil. God created a standard so that good could even be a possibility. God is also a loving God. He wants to love and He wants to be loved. If there were no standard to measure good and evil, then how would He be able to show His love to us? There would be no basis for measurement. In a sense, without that option of good or evil, God would have created robotic creatures without a choice. Who truly loves a robot? You need robots, but you do not love them. Once again, for God to have a basis to show His love, He had to give us a choice. God wants to be loved too. How could God give His creation the opportunity to love Him or not love Him without creating a choice to not love Him? Because He is a loving God who wants to show His love and receive His creation's love, He had to make that part of His creation.

It all started with Adam and Eve. He gave them free will and a choice. God created the possibility of both good and evil. Man makes the choice to enter into sin by not following the standard of holiness. Sin (or evil) would have no value unless there was a consequence. Following God's standards of good would have no value unless there was a consequence. These consequences of good and evil choices have to have a standard. Once again, without consequences of your choices, the standard would have no value. The consequences of the choice between evil (choosing to <u>not</u> obey God) and good (choosing to follow God's standards) are at least twofold. One of the consequences of sin deals with our eternal destiny. Will we go to heaven or to hell? I believe most everyone is aware of those consequences. While the first consequence deals with our disposition at death, the second deals with the quality of our lives while we are living. Our quality of life is driven in many ways by the joy received in our sense of self-fulfillment as well as our sense of identity while we participate in this process called life. Another dimension that deals with our quality of life is pain. Pain can have two purposes. One is used as a deterrent. If you do something wrong, the results may be painful. One thing is for sure — the consequence of sin is pain and usually the cause and effect is evident.

The other purpose of pain is this: In God's sovereign plan, there is another dimension of pain that is not a reflection of God's judgment but of part of His sovereign will. Only a Christian who is abiding in God can understand this truth. As strange as it may seem, pain can be a reflection of His love. A Christian who abides in God understands this and accepts that pain is often a reflection of His love. How can that be? Well, God now dwells within us and He uses people and varying circumstances to bring about His total plan. His ways are not our ways. So, we often do not understand the method and the need for pain in our lives. Remember a prevailing principle - some form of pain preceded almost all of man's and God's greatest accomplishments.

Question: Why does God use pain to accomplish His will? God relates differently to man now than He did during the old covenant. He works with His people through the principle of "giving and forgiving" to bring about change for the overall good of His pain. In the Old Testament, God most often used wars to bring about repentance, reverence, respect, and change. When His people were out of His will and ignored His call for repentance and change, He would send them into battle that resulted in defeat. The defeat would bring about his will. Now we are operating under a new covenant. To bring about change, God usually uses pain. He carefully chooses to honor a servant by asking him/her to endure hardship for the purpose of His plan so that all of His creation will benefit. He also did this in the old covenant.

Look at Job or Jonah. When a person abides in Christ, that person knows there is a purpose for that pain and discomfort and, therefore, it is okay. In fact, they should feel chosen. Actually, we have saints today in our community that are enduring pain and hardships for the glory of God and they understand the purpose for the pain.

Notice the transition from the old covenant to the new covenant. In the Old Testament, God used the pillow of fire to reveal Himself. Now He uses people, through the principle of "giving and forgiving" to reveal Himself through us to others.

Earlier, I said that God relates to men differently now than He did during the old covenant. How? I call it the Transformation. God's first covenant with man started with Noah, continued with Abraham and extended through with Moses. The first covenant (the Old Testament) was somewhat of a transactional relationship covenant. He gave His people the rules and laws of His creation, but He did not physically mingle among them. In fact, God could not be touched or even looked upon by man. Because God is holy and just, and because He cannot be in the presence of sin, He communicated with man through chosen priests at selected times. God is so holy that He cannot look upon sin nor can man look upon Him because of the existence of sin in man. Man's sin would defile a Holy God. Even God's chosen priests could not look upon Him. (As a point of interest, man was once able to look upon God but that was when man was sinless. Which man was once able to look upon the face of God? You've got it - Adam.) God gave his first chosen people the choice to follow Him through obedience or to deny him through disobedience. They disobeyed from the beginning, starting with Adam, and then stayed in disobedience. So, God brought Himself to earth through His Son, Jesus, so that He could walk in the midst of His creation and intermingle with man. Look at the transition and transformation. Where once man could not look upon God or even be in His presence, God came down through the incarnation of Jesus and walked among men. Can you see the transition of God stepping towards man, rather than man stepping towards God? Jesus also brought a new message and covenant. Now, instead of God having a transactional relationship with man from the outside in - through rituals and laws, He incarnated Himself in the form of His Son to bring about a new covenant that is a very personal relationship from the inside out. This new covenant was really an edification of the old covenant, but God brought in a new measuring stick of good and evil. Where once the measuring stick of good and evil was the law, now God puts within us, at the very least, a sense of good and evil as stated in Hebrews 8 vs. 6-10.

> *"But the ministry Jesus has received is as superior to theirs as the covenant of which he is mediator is superior to the old one, and it is founded on better promises.*
>
> *"For if there had been nothing wrong with that first covenant, no place would have been sought for another. But God found fault with the people and said:*
>
> *'The time is coming, declares the Lord, when I will make a new covenant with the House of Israel, and with the house of Judah.*
>
> *'It will not be like the covenant I made with their forefathers when I took them by the hand to lead them out of Egypt, because they did not remain faithful to my covenant, and I turned away from them, declares the Lord.*

This is the covenant I will make with the house of Israel after that time, declares the Lord.
I will put my laws in their minds and write them on their hearts.
I will be their God, and they will be my people'."

What an amazing God! Notice the transformation. Where once man could not look upon God, now man is able to walk with God through Jesus. During Jesus' life on earth, man could even touch God physically by touching Jesus. The last phase of the transformation is His indwelling through the Holy Spirit. That is where we are today. Because the Holy Spirit is within us, God is also within us and now we have a basic divine sense of God's right and wrong. (Romans 2, Hebrews 8) If you want to extend that relationship beyond a superficial relationship and really want to know the heart of God and the will of our Father, you will study His Word. If you want to totally abide in God, you have to know who He is. You can only know who God is by knowing His Word. To totally abide in Him is to know who you are and why you are here. If you study His Work and communicate with Him through prayer, God will reveal that to you.

In conclusion, the question comes back to the opening statement. How can a loving God allow pain, evil, and hell to exist? How can both good and evil coexist together in God's creation? My hypothesis is not to question <u>why</u> they both exist, but rather, how could they <u>not</u> both coexist in a loving God's plan? One cannot exist without the other. One justifies the other. It is incredible how God could be so brilliant to put into place such a unique and co-dependent program of balance and fairness to provide loving justice for all of His creation.

The second question that is a natural response to the first question is this: Does God condemn us to our pain and misery, or for that matter, to hell? The answer is: No, we condemn ourselves by virtue of the choices directed towards that end. We are not condemned to hell, but rather, our choice to accept or reject God's atonement in Jesus directs us to that end. How is it that we are able to have the ability to make that choice? God gave us a free will to make our own choices. However, there is a responsibility that goes along with a free choice. The responsibility is to accept the consequences of that choice. Even within the framework of our salvation experience, there are choices that God allows us to make. And there are repercussions to those choices. Good choices lead to good. Evil choices lead to evil. I am thankful that God made free will available at creation. Otherwise, my choices in life would have been made for me.

NOTE: In this discussion, I have used the term and concept of abiding or to be abiding in God (or in Christ). Let me clarify the intent in the use of these words. To abide in God means to merge with or to blend with. To be more specific, it means to blend with God in such a way that a new entity has been created that has its own character and identity and yet sustains the properties of the two separate entities used in the bonding process. In other words, when a person abides in Christ, a new person has been erected that has the nature and characteristics of Christ, through the Holy Spirit within. To illustrate this in a physical sense, solder (a substance used for bonding metals) is made of tin blended with lead. When these two elements are blended together, they form solder which has just the correct properties to accomplish an end that neither one could have independently accomplished on their own. SO, it is when we abide in God through Christ. Without abiding in God through Jesus, we could never have the knowledge, wisdom, strength, or desire to accomplish what we were created for. Without the resources of His people, God would not have the mechanism or vessel needed to accomplish His plan. As you can see, one is dependent on the other. Now, isn't that brilliant of God? Isn't that great? Oh, what a wonderful God!

Abiding in Christ might be the highest form of worship. Bruce Wilkinson in his book Secrets of the Vine gives a great discussion of the progressive forms of worship. He also believes that abiding in Christ is the highest form of worship.

One final note of interest I feel compelled to give. Have you ever considered your relative significance in all of creation? Just how important are you? Answer: God spoke into existence the entire universe with all of its laws and physical properties. Once again, He spoke the universe into existence. But when it came to man, He physically molded, shaped, and formed him into a likeness of His own image. The way I see it, your creation has far more value to Him than the entire universe. Your creation has even a deeper significance because you were created for a specific purpose, so say the Scriptures. Your ultimate joy will come when you abide in Him according to your calling.

CHAPTER 5 -

BLESSINGS AND MIRACLES

What an interesting subject. What is a blessing and/or miracle? Each term can be basically simple, but each can be made complex depending on the intent and application of the word. There are three methods to evaluate the intent and function of a word, or series of words: the theoretical, the philosophical and the theological. Listed below is a description of each:

Theoretical - A hypothesis (explanation) drawn from speculation. For this reason, theory is not used to study biblical terms and meanings.

Philosophical - A hypothesis drawn from what is believed to be truth or fact. There has to be a reason to believe some form of fact was used to derive the hypothesis. Philosophy can be used to study bible terms, but is most often not used. The reason why philosophy is not normally used is because most of the concepts used in the bible deal, to a large degree, with the element of faith. A large part of the Christian belief system is based on faith. If you are not a Christian, how can you explain the non-tangible power and force of the Holy Spirit? Faith is a key element in the Christian persuasion and that in itself excludes it from the definition of philosophical.

Theological - A hypothesis drawn from what is believed to be true from factual and non-factual evidence to derive a conclusion. The Christian faith derives conclusion from hard, irrefutable evidence and from evidences that are believed to be fact.

For the sake of this study, we will use the theological approach

Blessing, as defined in the Old Testament using the Hebrew word **brakah**, means "a benediction", or as defined in street talk language — a divine favor given by God on a person of His choice. This divine favor can come as a reward for obedience or the divine favor can come in the form of praise or approval. The most obvious application of this definition comes in Deuteronomy 11 vs. 26-28.

Deuteronomy 11 vs. 26-28

"See, I am setting before you today a blessing and a curse – the blessing if you obey the commands of the Lord your God that I am giving you today – the curse if you disobey the commands of the Lord your God

and turn from the way that I command you today by following other gods, which you have not known."

At this point, I want to draw an obvious conclusion when you use the Hebrew definition for blessing. Blessings come only from a divine origin. If you, by your own time and energy, cause or alter an event, most likely it is a function of your own ambition. God can bless you with the ability to do something to cause a desired event, but if you are not doing the event for god's sake or not following God's lead, it is probable the event is a function of your own ambition. Remember, God desires things to happen and he also allows things to happen. He may allow it, but He also may not desire it. Example from the Old Testament – God allowed Israel to have kings; He did not desire it. And it contributed to the spiritual leanness of the Israelites. Example from a present day situation – It is hard to say that God blessed me with a car, if the car was a function of my own self-serving desire. If it was, God did not bless me with the car; He allowed me to have it. It was my ambition to have the car, not His.

Some of God's blessings can be immediately understood and some blessings will be understood at a later time and some blessings may slip by us without us recognizing the blessing and other blessings cannot be understood immediately. God is in charge of all blessings, not man.

Miracles — miracles are blessings that are immediate and easily understood as a divine intervention of God. They have a desired outcome. Example — God ordains that a blind man can see or a cripple can walk. That blessing is immediate and easy to understand because it has a desired outcome. Do I believe in miracles — yes, yes, yes. God can choose to do what He desires. And it may not be what we approve of or understand. God does what He does for his own reasons. **What?** God does what He does for His own reasons? Yep. A clear testament to that fact is found in Romans 9. I challenge you to read the whole chapter.

Romans 9 vs. 14-16

> *"What then shall we say? Is God unjust? Not at all! For he says to Moses I will have mercy on whom I have mercy. It does not, therefore, depend on man's desire or effort, but on God's mercy".*

Going back to the subject of blessings, outlined below are some questions I have been challenged with regarding blessings, along with what I have derived from my study of the Scriptures on the subject:

WHAT DOES GOD CONSIDER THE MOST IMPORTANT BLESSING TO HIS PEOPLE?

The greatest blessing is that He dwells within us. Also, in Romans 10 vs. 15, Hebrews 9 vs.11 And Hebrews 10 vs.1, the goodness of God's blessing refers to the benefits provided through the sacrifice of Christ, in regard both to these things conferred through the gospel for all believers now and to those things which will come with thc Messianic Kingdom. In Psalm 3:8, God's blessing is upon His people through salvation.

WHAT IS KNOWN IS THE FIRST BLESSING?

The first occurrence of this blessing is when God blessed Abraham. God blesses those who are faithful to Him .

His Blessings bring:
... righteousness – Psalm 24 vs. 5
... life – Psalm 133 vs. 3
... salvation – Psalm 3 vs. 8
... prosperity – God can bless with possessions – II Samuel 7 vs. 29

DOES GOD BLESS US AT TIMES, AND WE DON'T RECOGNIZE IT?

Yes, more often than we realize, God is blessing us or has blessed us, and we missed it. How can that be? Remember, the blessing of a miracle is usually predictable and immediately desired and recognized. Other blessings come in a form that is unexpected. Example: The thing that brings God the most glory is when a person is not healed of some disease and he/she calls it a blessing because it has brought that person to a more intimate relationship with God. Case in point – Joni Erickson Tada.

Paralyzed from the waist down for over 30 years, she has gone from expecting and believing God for her healing to thankfulness that she was not healed because she knows God in a way she never would have if not paralyzed! Her ministry to others who are not healed brings God more glory than her healing would have. People don't like to hear or think of that. Far too often, Christians put conditions on God as to what would be a blessing and they try to transact with God in that manner. In essence, they say, **"If you love me, you will perform in the form of my expected behavior from You"** Another way a person tries to manipulate God is to say, **"Before I will consider it a blessing, this outcome should occur in the way I want it."** All you have to do is turn on the television set to hear this kind of false teaching being put forth.

Let me give an example of the greatest blessing to mankind that was messed up by God's own people. God promised His first chosen, the Jews, a Messiah, which would be the greatly-prophesized blessing. The blessing was that the Messiah was to be a conquering warrior. The Jews misjudged and predetermined the form of the Messiah and the form that was to be used to conquer. God sent Jesus, not as a warrior of war, who would shed the blood of others, but as a warrior of sacrifice, who would give His own blood for others. As it says in the book of Hebrews, conquering by war did not work. Jesus came to set a new standard and a new method. His people will conquer by love through giving and forgiving. The first chosen, the Jews, missed the blessing of the promised Messiah because they had predetermined what they would receive as a blessing. Because of this, they have never had the gifts of joy or peace. That should be a clear lesson for us all to learn. God is blessing us every day. Our joy, peace and sense of self-worth is directly correlated to our belief in that. Remember, the greatest blessing that we as Christians have ever received is when God came to live within each of us through the Person of the Holy Spirit. If that was the only blessing we would ever receive, it would be enough.

WHAT ARE OUR EXPECTATIONS AND PERCEPTIONS OF BLESSINGS?

The Lord has allowed me to visit many other countries on mission trips. When I return, I am amazed to see once again how God has set this land in the United States of America apart from the rest of the world and allowed it to be blessed. I know in my heart of hearts that this land was blessed because it was founded on Christian principles. The name and Word of God was woven into every legal document. God's name even appears on our currency. That same blessing has not shown up in any other country. What we take for granted here in the USA would be considered a blessing anywhere outside the borders of the USA. What is considered a poverty and waste here in the USA is considered a blessing in most other countries. I have been in many church services in Central and South America where the people were thanking God for things like a glass of clean water, a half-spoiled apple, or a piece of tin metal they could use as shelter and considered them blessings. Many of these people are diseased, tired and hungry, but yet, they find joy, peace, contentment and a sense of self-worth because they give thanks for all things and consider all things a gift or blessing from God. Because of what I have seen, my life has been changed and I try to be thankful for even the smallest things that life has to offer. I have the ability to make a choice. I will choose to consider all things as a blessing from God. I choose to be grateful for what God allows me to have, rather than to murmur over what I do not have. The most special blessing to me is that the Holy Spirit lives within me.

CONCLUSION

It has been fun and enlightening to study what God considers as a blessing. I have found that many individuals have used the term and concept of blessing as a tool to justify their own greed and self-gratification. The hypothesis or thought process goes like this — God must love me because the more He loves me, the more He gives me for my own self-indulgence. That may have been true under the first covenant, but it is not so true under the New Covenant. Under the New Covenant, all blessings are given to glorify His name, not our name. We are to use those gifts and blessings to show His love to others, by His people, through giving and forgiving. We as Christians should find joy, peace and a sense of divine purpose because He is in control. Therefore, there are three things that should be derived from all blessings and miracles. God does blessings and miracles in our lives for three reasons. The three reasons are:

- Righteousness - knowing what God values as right and wrong and knowing God's will for our life to serve His purpose
- Holiness - doing God's will for good and his purpose
- Intimacy - God wants to have an intimate love relationship with His people

CHAPTER 6 -

WHAT COULD ANGER JESUS?

As you read the accounts of Jesus while He walked the earth, you can see a man who was filled with passion for His people. There are accounts where He wept for the sick and even the dead. There is an account where He wept over Jerusalem. There are accounts where He healed the helpless. There are accounts where He did not judge a person's sin but rather forgave the sin and said, 'sin no more'. His passion for His people was so great, that one day He went to the cross to fulfill and pay the blood price required by the Original Law. Even though He did not commit any sin, He chose to offer His blood to pay the blood price for all past, present, and future sins to satisfy the requirement of the Original Law. ***The Original Law — because of Adam's sin, blood must be given to cover all sin***. Incidentally, that law has never been repealed, even though some would like to think it has.

Now, knowing all this —What could cause Jesus to get angry? There are four instances that I could find that caused Jesus to be angry and there is a common thread that runs through all three. ***That common thread is a lack of compassion shown by those in authority to His people. The lack of***

compassion was driven by a need for power and control by using the tools of legalism and hypocrisy.

Hypocrisy — is the pretense of having possessions of feelings or characteristics that one does not possess, especially, the deceitful assumption of praiseworthy qualities. Hypocrisy denotes a presumption of admirable qualities such as goodness, sincerity, and honesty by those who actually have the opposite qualities. Since they are unwilling to practice the very qualities that they aspire to, it becomes a practice of dishonesty and deceptiveness. It is a disguise of the real truth and heart of the person. In street talk it is simply said this way: You ain't what you say you are.

Legalism — the Pharisees, as well as many others here on earth today, used the Word of God in a legalistic manner to create envy, a deception of religiousness and to have control and power over other people's lives. Knowledge of the Scriptures can become a tool for self-elevation by making others of less knowledge feel inferior or inadequate. Knowledge can be a powerful tool to gain control over other people's lives. Eventually these people become "self-proclaimed doctrinal priests". They ignore the intent and purpose of the teachings of Jesus and turn those teachings into an instrument of destruction. Jesus was all about showing love and humility through **giving** and **forgiving**. Power can have a contrived force and this force does not usually lend itself to the acts of **giving** and **forgiving**.

Now, let us analyze those three instances:

Jesus was provoked to anger as recorded in Mark 3 vs. 1-6

"Another time he went into the synagogue, and a man with a shriveled hand was there. Some of them were looking for a reason to accuse Jesus, so they watched him closely to see if he would heal him on the Sabbath. Jesus said to the man with the shriveled hand, 'Stand up in front of everyone'. Then Jesus asked them, 'Which is lawful on the Sabbath: to do good or to do evil, to save a life or to kill?' But they remained silent. He looked around at them in anger and deeply distressed at their stubborn hearts, said to the man, 'Stretch out your hand.' He stretched it out, and his hand was completely restored. Then the Pharisees went out and began to plot with the Herodians how they might kill Jesus."

As the record states, Jesus had mercy on a man in need. He felt compassion for the man. Jesus met the man at His most important need. He healed the shriveled hand. The Jewish leaders of the synagogue stood on the law to refuse compassion. They refused to yield to the purpose of the law which then made the law a curse to man rather than a blessing to man. That in fact, is hypocrisy and it angered Jesus as is demonstrated in verse 5.

"He looked around at them in anger and deeply distressed at their stubborn hearts, said to the man,

> *'Stretch out your hand.' He stretched it out and his hand was completely restored."*

Jesus again was provoked to anger as recorded in Matthew 23, vs. 13-37. Jesus was provoked to anger by the Pharisees because of their hypocrisy and legalism. These verses are commonly referred to as the "Seven woes of Jesus".

Matthew 23 vs. 13-37

> *"Woe to you, teachers of the law and Pharisees, you hypocrites! You shut the kingdom of heaven in men's faces. You yourselves do not enter, nor will you let those enter who are trying to. Woe to you, teachers of the law and Pharisees, you hypocrites! You travel over land and sea to win a single convert, and when he becomes one, you make him twice as much a son of hell as you are. Woe to you, blind guides! You say, 'If anyone swears by the temple, it means nothing; but if anyone swears by the gold of the temple, he is bound by his oath.' You blind fools! Which is greater: the gold, or the temple that makes the gold sacred? You also say, 'If anyone swears by the altar, it means nothing; but if anyone swears by the gift on it, he is bound by his oath.' You blind men! Which is greater: the gift, or the altar that makes the gift sacred? Therefore, he who swears by the altar swears by it and by everything on it. And he who swears by the temple swears by it and by the One who dwells in it. And he who swears by heaven swears by God's throne and by the one who sits on it.*

> *"Woe to you, teachers of the law and the Pharisees, you hypocrites! You give a tenth of your spices –*

mint, dill and cummin. But you have neglected the more important matters of the law — justice, mercy and faithfulness. You should have practiced the latter, without neglecting the former. You blind guides! You strain out a gnat but swallow a camel. Woe to you, teachers of the law and Pharisees, you hypocrites! You clean the outside of the cup and dish, but inside they are full of greed and self-indulgence. Blind Pharisee! First clean the inside of the cup and dish and then the outside also will be clean. Woe to you teachers of the law and Pharisees, you hypocrites! You are like whitewashed tombs, which look beautiful on the outside but on the inside are full of dead men's bones and everything unclean. In the same way, on the outside you appear to people as righteous but on the inside you are full of hypocrisy. Woe to you, teachers of the law and Pharisees, you hypocrites! You build tombs for the prophets and decorate the graves of the righteous. And you say, 'If we had lived in the days of our forefathers, we would not have taken part with them in shedding the blood of the prophets .' So you testify against yourselves that you are the descendants of those who murdered the prophets. Fill up, then the measure of sin of your forefathers!

"You snakes! You brood of vipers! How will you escape being condemned to hell? Therefore I am sending you prophets and wise men and teachers. Some of them you will kill and crucify; others you will flog in your synagogues and pursue from town to town. And so upon you will come all the righteous blood that has been shed on earth, from the blood of righteous Abel to the blood of Zechariah son of Berakiah, whom you murdered between the temple

and the altar. I tell you the truth, all this will come upon this generation.

"O Jerusalem, Jerusalem, you who kill the prophets and stone those sent to you, how often I have longed to gather your children together, as a hen gathers her chicks under her wings, but you were not willing. Look, your house is left to you desolate. For I tell you, you will not see me again until you say, 'Blessed is he who comes in the name of the Lord'."

Read this scripture and then reread it carefully. What could you or I or anyone add to Jesus' reaction to the Pharisees and keepers of the law? It is clear, Jesus has no tolerance for hypocrisy and teachers of the law who do not show compassion for the less fortunate. That same attitude and passion is shown in Matthew 25 vs. 31-46, when Jesus said "When you have done it unto to the least of these, you have done it unto me." Jesus has put a command upon His people to help and care for one another and to especially care for the less fortunate and those who need help.

The third record of Jesus being angered was at the temple. There are two accounts of this incidence, Mark 11 vs. 15-18 and Matthew 21 vs. 12-13.

Mark 11 vs. 15-18

"On reaching Jerusalem, Jesus entered the temple area and began driving out those who were buying and selling there. He overturned the tables of the money changers and the benches of those selling doves, and would not allow anyone to carry merchandise through the temple courts. And as he taught them, he said, 'Is it not written: My house will

be called a house of prayer for all nations'? But you have made it a den of robbers.

"The chief priests and the teachers of the law heard this and began looking for a way to kill him, for they feared him, because the whole crowd was amazed at his teaching."

Matthew 21 vs. 12-13

"Jesus entered the temple area and drove out all who were buying and selling there. He overturned the tables of the money changers and the benches of those selling doves. It is written, he said to them, My house will be called a house of prayer,' but you are making it a den of robbers'."

The temple (the place of worship) signified a place of rest, peace and reverence, not a place of commerce. The church – the place of worship today is often used as a social center to create perceptions and illusions for social and/or business purposes. Yes, I said business purposes. These same people can also use the church to gain and give the perception of spirituality. **That is called hypocrisy.** Because, the presumption is that you are going to church for worship purposes, but the church occasion is used for other purposes. Many times in our own church I can overhear people discussing and communicating business transactions during a time that should be held in preparation for holiness. Maybe you have seen this happen in your church as well or, even worse, you yourself are guilty of the same thing.

A fourth record of Jesus being angered also involved hypocrisy, as well as legalism. It is found in Matthew. Matthew 15 vs. 1-9 (The Living Bible)

"Some Pharisees and other Jewish leaders now arrived from Jerusalem to interview Jesus. 'Why do your disciples break the tradition of the elders? They don't wash their hands before they eat!" Jesus replied, 'And why do your traditions violate the direct commands of God. For instance, God's law is to honor your father and mother; anyone who reviles his parents must die.' But you say, 'Even if your parents are in need, you may give their support money to the church instead.' And so, by your man-made rule, you disobey the direct command of God to honor and care for your parents. You hypocrites! Well did Isaiah prophesy of you:

'These people say that they honor me, but their hearts are far from me. Their Worship is worthless."

All of us can be guilty of this hypocrisy – using one good act which pleases God to justify overlooking another good act which pleases God more. The Pharisees felt righteous in that they were giving money as an offering to God. But, they were doing it at the expense of helping their own parents. This angered Jesus to the point of calling them hypocrites. They neglected what was more important for a lesser work. Perhaps there were unresolved issues with their parents which made it easier to help the poor and needy. They might have been justified. Nevertheless, Jesus did not excuse them. In fact, he became very angry with them.

This is an area we can all fall short in. Some may even claim that "Honor thy Father and Mother" is part of the Old Covenant. However, Jesus, who had just ushered in the New Covenant, made it clear that honoring their father and mother came first before honoring and helping others. In writing about what angered God and including this fourth record of Jesus being angered, I saw something for the first time. Jesus was very angry that these Pharisees had not honored their parents. Think with me for a moment. What was the source of Jesus' anger when he drove out the money changers, buyers and sellers from the Temple? He said that His father's house was to be a house of prayer. They had not honored His father. Now, there is a common problem between both of these incidents. – not honoring parents. In the same way that He was angered with the Pharisees for neglecting their parents, He is angry when we do not honor our father and mother. And that honor is not contingent on whether or not they deserve it. I wonder how often we also at times do not honor our parents and so "nullify the word of God." I wonder how often, when we do not honor our parents, that we honor God with our lips but our heart is far from Him?

CONCLUSION

Our Holy Father loves His creations and His people. He showed that love with His Son Jesus at the cross. God sent His only son to reveal the only way that man can live in total harmony is through ***giving*** and ***forgiving.*** Our Holy Father likes the "real thing" not a perception or an illusion of the "real thing". He does not like hypocrisy. God wants passion and compassion over the structure of the law and hypocrisy.

Everybody has a concept and a value and an expectation from God the Father, Jesus the Son and the Holy Spirit. The bigger question is this — What do you think the Trinity's expectation is of you? — What is it? I like to keep little phrases in mind to help guide me. One phrase is this — ***What displeases God the most is not what has not been done for the sake of God but rather what has been done for the sake of self.*** He wants us **to give** and **forgive** as a desire to demonstrate our love for Him.

You have had a chance to read and review what has angered God. As you think about your relationship and walk with Jesus, do you have any reason to believe that your walk would provoke anger in our Lord?

CHAPTER 7 –

I NEED HELP

Have you ever been in a situation where you have felt so alone? Where you have felt nobody understood your problems or cared about your problems? Where the problem is bigger than any possible solution? Where even God appears to have abandoned you? You want to make a cry, "I Need Help"! The problem of being desperate and needing help is not a modern day problem. It dates back to the beginning of time.

The Bible records accounts where people were enraptured by overpowering problems. Some of the problems were psychological, some mental, some self-imposed and some spiritual. Regardless of the reason for the problem, it was still a problem and the Bible records that they made a cry, "I Need Help!" Those people may not have used those particular words, but that was the intent of their cry, "I Need Help!" Let us examine a few of those accounts.

NOTE: Before we examine the accounts, it is important to make a distinction of word meanings. The word Lord and Son of David is used many times. Examine the text and meanings of these words.

Lord* - -**The word Lord is used in many places and is connected to the name and the person of Jesus. Most people assume that the word "lord" has the same meaning as Messiah, of which it does not. The word "lord" in the Hebrew (the language of the day) meant 'One who has great power or authority'. The word "Lord" was used later in the New Testament as "Master or Owner". At the time of Jesus, they did not know Jesus as their Messiah, but only as one who had power or authority, ***a lord. It was only after the resurrection that Jesus was truly known as the Messiah. ***Son of David*** **-** It was very common to refer to someone as a descendant of someone else. Since Jesus was a descendant of David it would be natural, and almost expected to refer to him as Jesus, (Son) descendant of David.

Matthew 9 vs. 20-22 - A Cry for Help—Woman With Internal Bleeding

> *"Just then a woman who had been subject to bleeding for twelve years came up behind him and touched the edge of his cloak. She said to herself, 'If I only touch his cloak, I will be healed'. Jesus turned and saw her.' Take heart, daughter,' he said, 'your faith has healed you'. And the woman was healed from that moment".*

Here is an example of a woman who had a serious problem for 12 years. I am sure she cried for help for 12 years, but nothing could be done. Finally, she recognized a person with great power and cried out to Jesus as a lord, saying – "I Need Help", in a manner of speaking.

Matthew 9 vs. 27-31 - A Cry For Help From Two Blind Men

> *"As Jesus went on from there, two blind men followed him, calling out, 'Have mercy on us, Son of David!'.*

When he had gone indoors, the blind men came to him, and he asked them, 'Do you believe that I am able to do this'? 'Yes Lord,' they replied. Then he touched their eyes and said, 'According to your faith will it be done to you', and their sight was restored. Jesus warned them sternly, 'See that no one knows about this'. But they went out and spread the news about him all over the region."

This story tells of two blind men who had a problem that was out of their control. They also knew that the solution to their problems could only be dealt with by a lord. They followed Jesus and asked for mercy. Jesus said, "Do you believe that I am able to do this?" They said, "Yes, Lord" referring to the one who has great power — Jesus heard their cry of — I Need Help, and exercised and demonstrated His power by healing them.

Matthew 15 vs. 22-28 - A Cry For Help From A Mother

Whose Daughter Was Demon Possessed

"A Canaanite woman from that vicinity came to him, crying out, 'Lord, Son of David, have mercy on me! My daughter is suffering from a terrible demon-possession.' Jesus did not answer a word. So his disciples came to him and urged him, 'Send her away for she keeps crying out after us'. He answered, 'I was sent only to the lost sheep of Israel.' The woman came and knelt before him. 'Lord, help me!' she said. He replied, 'It is not right to take the children's bread and toss it to their dogs.' 'Yes, Lord,' she said, 'but even the dogs eat the crumbs that fall from their master's table.' Then Jesus answered, 'Woman, you have great faith! Your request is granted.' And her

daughter was healed from that very hour".

This mother must have been desperate. Can you imagine the hopelessness she must have felt? She also did not know Jesus as the Messiah, but Jesus as a lord. Sometimes when life's circumstances seem so helpless and Jesus the Messiah does not seem to be there, you have to cry out – "Lord, I Need Help", just as she did. "I Need Help".

Matthew 17 vs. 14-16 -A Cry For Help From A Man Whose Son Had Seizures

> *"When they came to the crowd, a man approached Jesus and knelt before him. 'Lord, have mercy on my son,' he said. 'He is an epileptic and is suffering greatly. He often falls into the fire or into the water. I brought him to your disciples, but they could not heal him'."*

Here is an account of a man who seemed to have a problem that was bigger than any known solution. He cried out, "Lord (one who has power) have mercy on my son." He had heard enough to know Jesus was a lord, but wouldn't it have been wonderful if he had known him as the Messiah? That distinction of Messiah was yet to come.

Many of us know Jesus as Lord and as the Messiah and as Our Savior, but even knowing all of this, we can feel so abandoned and alone. Sometimes there's nothing left to do but cry out – "I Need Help." Jesus will hear your cry. You may not be able to predict or recognize His response immediately, but He will respond immediately. The actions of His response may not be seen until later.

Mark 2 vs. 1-9 - A Cry For Help From The Friends Of A Paralyzed Man

"A few days later, when Jesus again entered Capernaum, the people heard that he had come home. So many gathered that there was no room left, not even outside the door, and he preached the word to them. Some men came, bringing to him a paralytic, carried by four of them. Since they could not get him to Jesus because of the crowd, they made an opening in the roof above Jesus and, after digging through it, lowered the mat the paralyzed man was lying on. When Jesus saw their faith, he said to the paralytic, 'Son, your sins are forgiven.' Now some teachers of the law were sitting there, thinking to themselves, 'Why does this fellow talk like that? He's blaspheming! Who can forgive sins but God alone?'

"Immediately Jesus knew in his spirit that this was what they were thinking in their hearts, and he said to them, 'Why are you thinking these things? Which is easier: to say to the paralytic, 'Your sins are forgiven,' or to say, 'Get up, take up your mat and walk'? But that you may know that the Son of Man has authority on earth to forgive sins...He said to the paralytic, 'I tell you, get up, take your mat and go home.' He got up, took his mat and walked out in full view of them all. This amazed everyone and they praised God, saying, 'We have never seen anything like this'."

Here is an account where many men recognized the Lordship of Jesus and made a cry for help, "I Need Help."

A NOTE ON THE HEALINGS DONE BY JESUS

Jesus did healing freely during his walk on earth to demonstrate the power given to him by His Holy Father.

This power was given to demonstrate and to establish His role and position of not only Lord, but also, as a prelude to His ultimate role as the Messiah — The Son of God.

While Jesus walked on earth, He was God/Man. Once He was crucified, He gave up His earthly role and became God/Savior. The method, purpose, function and intention of the healings done as God/Man (while Jesus walked on earth) were done for a different reason than after the resurrection and ascension when He became God/Savior. The act that established Him as the Messiah happened at resurrection and ascension. The event of resurrection and ascension validated all that He taught. One of His major roles was to come as a teacher to reveal the last and ultimate truth that would ever be given to man. **Now**, as for the healings done after the resurrection and ascension as God/Savior. I personally believe from all that I have read and all that I know about the healings done under the new dispensation and the New Covenant, the healings are, for the most part, done for three reasons. The reasons are these:

- Righteousness - knowing what God values as right and wrong and knowing God's will for our life to serve His purpose
- Holiness - doing God's will for our good and his purpose
- Intimacy - God wants to have an intimate love relationship with His people

Jesus did healing freely to demonstrate the power given to Him by the Lord, for the purpose of establishing His role and position as the Messiah - the Son of God. These healings were all done before the resurrection and his ascension into heaven. Healings done after the resurrection and ascension have a whole different purpose, function and designated intention and that is to establish within each of us, the properties of righteousness, holiness and intimacy.

CONCLUSION

The Bible records many, many instances where many people made a cry for help. What I have illustrated is only a few.

"I Need Help" - Have you ever been there? Are you there now? Does it seem as if nobody understands or cares about your hurts? You may be a Christian and you may be wondering, "God, if you loved me, how could you let me suffer like this?" In a previous chapter, you read ***A RATIONALE FOR THE EXISTENCE OF GOOD AND EVIL*** THAT DISCUSSES THIS TOPIC. Well, the answer is not simple, but the answer is sure and absolute. <u>JESUS IS ALWAYS THERE.</u> We may not always feel His presence but He is always there. During the time of His walk on earth, Jesus did a lot of physical, emotional and spiritual healings. He did that to establish His Lordship to help justify Himself as the ultimate role He would assume as Messiah. Those healings were very evident, easy to understand and served the purpose for that time. Jesus is still in the business of healing, but the purpose and the motive may be different.

At this point stay with me while I give a rationale for my next proposition. In the first covenant God came to man and man was required to obey out of duty. When Adam sinned in the Garden, God put a barrier between Himself and man and required a blood offering for redemption of sin. Then God made His first contractual agreement with man through Moses. From there, the Old Testament was established. God chose to use intercessors or ambassadors to communicate with His people, rather than dealing with all of His people on an individual basis. The first covenant (the Old Testament) did not work, so God sent Jesus to earth to be the example and to set the standard for His New Covenant, which is revealed through the New Testament. He also sent Jesus to introduce the Holy Spirit. Because of this, God's role and relationship with man changed. In the Old Covenant, God conquered through wars as a method to demonstrate His authority, power and as a discipline tool for His people. Since none of this worked, He changed His method. God did an amazing thing then. He sent Jesus. Instead of keeping a barrier between Himself and man, God stepped toward man and became very intimate with man through Jesus and used the blood of Jesus to cover the sin debt. God stepped toward man again and gave Himself to live within man through the power of the Holy Spirit and now He dwells within us in the form of the Holy Spirit. As I said, under the Old Covenant He conquered by war. Now under the New Covenant, He conquers by love through the power of giving and forgiving.

Next Proposition – Please consider all of the above as a rationale for a new thought process. The events and circumstances we as humans view as problems may in fact be the very mechanism that God can use to serve his purpose to fulfill His plan for the good of mankind. Remember, we as humans have a finite mind and God doesn't. We as Christians must come to see that God is not part of our plans, but rather Christians are part of His plan.

Let me give you an example of how a person can fulfill God's plan and purpose through the suffering and even death of a loving and privileged person. This person made a tremendous impact on the lives of countless other people. My mother died by a very slow death process. She died at age 58 from cancer. She never complained

> and was always concerned about the well being of others during her whole dying process. The way she handled this dying process and eventually her death, impacted my life beyond measure and did the same for countless others. The witness of her life has rippled down through two other generations. I would venture to say it altered the lives of hundreds and maybe even thousands. Did she suffer? Yes - very much. Did she have pain? Yes? - very much. Did she complain?
> No - not that I can remember. She was a born-again Christian and she knew her witness had a greater value than her own life. Has God used her pain and suffering for His greater purpose? Yes, yes, yes. Her flesh may be dead, but her spirit and memory lives on.

Look at what happened to Jesus for the sake of our Holy Father's plans. Look at John the Baptist. Look at all of the prophets. Look at all of the disciples. They all suffered greatly and they died for the sake of our Holy Father. Now, let us consider our cries. Most of the time our cries, "I Need Help", are for the sake of our self. Most of the time our cry should be "How can I Help?", rather than "I Need Help", or our cry should be "I Need Help TO DO YOUR WILL". Jesus is still in the business of helping and healing. It may not always come in the form we think we want or understand. Jesus is still in the business of healing. Remember, Jesus will do what is necessary to serve all of His creation; Jesus will do what is necessary to refine our righteousness and holiness so that we might serve Him. A lot of times that involves suffering and people do not like suffering.

Remember the next time we make that cry "I Need Help", let's try three more words – "To Serve You". If you are not a Christian, just make the cry "I Need Help". God will help you because He created you and He loves you and He wants you to be a part of His glorious plan so that you can live in glory for eternity. He sent His Son to fulfill His plan for you.

King David made a cry for help, too. While his time was before the life of Jesus Christ on earth, he also cried out to the Lord, "I need help". Check out Psalms 61 and 62. David had previously been pursued by King Saul who, out of jealousy, wanted to take his life. Now David's son, Absalom, was warring against him for his kingdom. David's life covered the whole spectrum. He began as a poor shepherd boy, slew the Philistine giant Goliath, and was elevated to being a powerful king over all of Israel. Now, he is old, tired and vulnerable. He makes a plea to the Lord for help. "I need help". David came to find the ultimate peace, solitude and assurance in His Father God. Psalm 62 vs. 1,2 and vs. 8 express it clearly. This same assurance is also offered to us by God our Father through His son Jesus Christ.

Psalm 62 vs. 1,2

> *"My soul finds rest in God alone; my salvation comes from him. He alone is my rock and my salvation; he is my fortress. I will never be shaken."*

Psalm 62 vs. 8

> *"Trust in him at all times, O people; pour out your hearts to him, for God is our refuge."*

CHAPTER 8 -

ACTS OF FORGIVENESS

Wrong deeds can be forgiven in one of two ways. The Bible says that Jesus is the only mediator between God and man, and that God is the only one who can forgive sins. Through His shed blood, Jesus provided the way for man to go directly to God and ask forgiveness for his sins. A human being can forgive offenses done to each other, but only God can forgive the sin of the wrongdoing.

In my discussions with believers of certain religions, I have asked how the institutionalized priest, pastor, or church leader can forgive sin. Their responses differ. Some believe the leader can actually forgive the sin. There are some that believe Mary (the mother of Jesus) can forgive sin. Others quote their leader as teaching that a priest, pastor, or church leader cannot forgive sin itself. However, by the confession of sin to the leader and the leader's committing the sin is forgiven, then the sin is forgiven. The church leader justifies this position by Paul's act of forgiveness in II Corinthians. 2: vs. 10, "If you forgive him, I will also forgive him." If you read the scriptures, you will see that Paul was not speaking in the text of sin against God. He was literally referring to ungodly offenses against another person. And he said, "If you people forgive him, so will I." A man had committed incest. Paul rebuked him. The man corrected his wrongs but his shame was causing him anguish and affliction. Paul was asking the Corinthians to help and love him. And he went on to say, "If you forgive him, so will I."

Teaching that any mortal man (be it priest, pastor or leader) can forgive sin can be dangerous to the souls of people. Only God can forgive sin. God forgives sin by grace through the spilled blood of Jesus Christ.

FORGIVING OTHERS

Perhaps one of the most difficult commands of Jesus is to forgive others "from the heart". To forgive "from the heart" means to forgive in the same way that God has forgiven us. Do we really understand what it means **to forgive "from the heart"**? The following scripture refers to an example:

Matthew 18 vs. 21-35

> *"Then Peter came to Jesus and asked, 'Lord, how many times shall I forgive my brother when he sins against me? Up to seven times'? Jesus answered, 'I tell you, not seven times, but seventy-seven times. Therefore, the kingdom of heaven is like a king who wanted to settle accounts with his servants. As he began the settlement, a man who owed him ten thousand talents was brought to him. Since he was not able to pay, the master ordered that he and his wife and his children and all that he had to be sold to repay the debt. The servant fell on his knees before him. 'Be patient with me' he begged, 'and I will pay back everything.' The servant's master took pity on him, canceled the debt and let him go. But when the servant went out, he found one of his fellow servants who owed him a hundred denarii. He grabbed him*

> *and began to choke him. 'Pay back what you owe me!' he demanded. His fellow servant fell to his knees and begged him, 'Be patient with me, and I will pay you back.' But he refused. Instead, he went off and had the man thrown into prison until he could pay the debt. When the other servants saw what had happened, they were greatly distressed and went and told their master everything that had happened. Then the master called the servant in. 'You wicked servant,' he said, 'I canceled all that debt of yours because you begged me to. Shouldn't you have had mercy on your fellow servant just as I had mercy on you?' In his anger his master turned him over to the jailers until he should pay back all he owed. This is how my heavenly Father will treat each of you unless you forgive your brother from your heart."*

Notice how Jesus referred to the man who did not forgive – verse 32 – "You wicked servant". Question – Does Jesus view us as a wicked servant if we do not forgive? Then Jesus says in verse 35, "forgive your brother from the heart".

The New Testament Greek word for "forgiveness" literally means "to let go", to "send away", or to "cancel a debt owed". Letting go is very hard when we have been offended. We naturally want to hold fast to our need to get even, to our "right" to be angry. Anger, for a season, may feel good. But, the "feel good" soon goes away and a person is left with bitterness. Bitterness is what holds us captive and will control the joy of the day and the hope of tomorrow. If this downward spiral is left unchecked, it will lead to depression and can ultimately lead to suicide. Forgiveness from the heart is the only provision God has for the healing of the emotional wounds of anger and bitterness brought on by offenses of any kind.

Many times we think we have forgiven someone because he/she has hurt us. We think we have forgiven him/her, but have we really forgiven them? The thought of the offense still stirs up hurt and anger. The hurt or anger stirred up is evidence that the forgiveness was not "from the heart". What does "from the heart" mean? Ephesians 4:32 tells us that we are to forgive just as "God, in Christ, has forgiven you". From studying the scriptures on how God forgives, you will find that God forgave us

... while we were still sinning
... before we admitted our sin
... before we asked for forgiveness
... completely
... unconditionally (holding back nothing from us)

Most offenses come in the form of verbal criticism or accusations. What do we do when offended in this manner? Our example must be from Jesus. In I Peter 2:23 we read these words on offenses:

> *"When they hurled their insults at Jesus, He did not retaliate; when he suffered, he made no threats. Instead, he entrusted himself to him who judges justly."*

In other words, Jesus trusted God to be his defender and did not try to defend Himself. We are instructed to do likewise all through the Bible. In Proverbs 19 vs. 11 we read these words:

> *"It is to a man's glory to overlook an offense."*

What does it mean to "overlook" an offense? Does it mean that we deny the offense occurred? Does it mean we deny the pain caused by the offense? No. To "overlook" an offense is to "hardly notice" as some translations state. To "hardly notice" is to admit the hurt and pain of the offense to God, being honest with our feelings. Then we are to forgive and release the offense and not think on it again. These are hard teachings. Our human nature is to defend ourselves when we are accused or offended. We do not want to suffer wrong. The following scriptures give instructions as to what paves the way to overlooking an offense:

Colossians 3 vs. 13a

> *"You must make allowances for each other's faults, and forgive the person who offends you."*

In this verse we are told to "make allowances" for other's faults. In other words, "give the person some slack". After making allowances for their faults and choosing to overlook the offense, we are ready to forgive that person.

In the verses preceding the verse on Jesus' response to insults, we find further instruction on being offended or wronged.

I Peter 2 vs. 19-22

> *"For it is commendable if a man bears up under the pain of unjust suffering because he is conscious of God. But how is it to your credit if you receive a beating for doing wrong and endure it? But if you suffer for doing good and you endure it, this is commendable before God. To this you were called, because Christ suffered for you, leaving you an example, that you should follow in his steps."*

Many times you will hear someone say something like "I have forgiven so and so, but I will not be around him any more". That attitude shows that the forgiveness was not "from the heart" as God requires. Question - How does God treat us after He has forgiven us, when we sin? It is as if the sin had never happened! Wow!! A good test to see if you really have forgiven someone who has wronged you is to examine how you treat that person. Do you withhold love or kindness from that person? Do you withdraw, either emotionally or physically? If so, then you have not forgiven "from the heart". Forgiveness "from the heart" brings about God's grace to love and to be kind to those who hurt us. Question - Is this hard to do? - Yes, but with the help of Jesus, it can be done.

Matthew 18 vs. 21-15 tells us when we do not forgive as God forgives us, He will send the tormentors. That seems harsh. But, forgiveness is the message of the Cross and God will do what He must do to bring us to forgiveness "from the heart". He does this out of His love for us. Forgiveness is for the one who has been offended.

Dr. Chuck Swindoll, noted pastor, author and teacher, says this about forgiveness:

> "The escape route out of the prison of bitterness is clearly marked. It leads to the cross — where the only One who had a right to be bitter — wasn't."

He also says this about forgiveness:

> "There is no torment like the inner torment of an unforgiving spirit. I am convinced that a person is far more miserable in his own bitterness than he was by the offense which caused the bitterness to develop. When you forgive, you throw wide the prison doors and then realize that the prisoner was —You!"

Why is forgiveness so hard? **Consider this** — for the most part people are pretty selfish and self-serving. Most of what is considered an offense that needs forgiveness is because somebody did not do something the way I wanted it done or whatever was done did not serve me the way I wanted to be served. Simply stated, most offenses become offenses because I want it my way and it did not go my way. A true servant is hardly ever offended, which requires no forgiveness. A person who wants to be served is easily offended and demands forgiveness. **The next** and most important reason that forgiveness is so hard is because, as mentioned earlier, forgiveness is the message of the cross. Satan knows that and will do all that he can to prevent forgiveness "from the heart". Jesus is the only one who tells us we can forgive ... but... Satan hates forgiveness from the heart because Jesus, on the cross, forgave from His heart. On the cross, Jesus asked God to forgive the very ones who crucified Him. (And that included you and me, not just the Roman soldiers.) They did not ask for nor deserve that forgiveness. Because Jesus did that for us, it grieves the heart of God when we won't forgive "from our hearts". Satan can also use our pride to try to hinder us from completely forgiving. Pride can be at the root of all conditional forgiveness. Forgiveness from the heart takes time, especially when the hurt has been severe and continual. However, it begins with the choice to forgive. Each time, the hurt surfaces and bitterness wants to set in, the choice to forgive has to be repeated. Eventually, Satan leaves us alone and forgiveness from the heart is complete.

There is one aspect of Jesus' forgiveness of his slayers while he was on the cross that is often missed. Consider His words: "Father, forgiven them <u>for they know not what they do</u>." (Underlining mine.) From a pragmatic point of view, what Jesus was literally saying referred to the fact that his accusers were crucifying the very thing that they had prayed for. For years, they had prayed for a messiah, and now they were crucifying the very thing they had prayed for. It is interesting, however, to know how God can use the same scriptures to impact people differently. For instance, my wife had an experience some years ago in which this scripture was what God used to enable her to forgive an offense. I want to share that with you:

Several years ago, someone very close to my wife had treated her in such a way that was very insensitive and brought the pain of being hurt. As most often happens, the hurt turned to anger. The afternoon of that same day, my wife had a doctor's appointment. Her doctor was a Christian who had various Christian pictures and scriptures hung in her waiting room and examining rooms. As my wife was in one of the examining rooms waiting for the doctor to come in, she was still hurting and angry. She looked up, and on the wall right in front of her was a picture of Jesus on the cross. Beneath the cross were the words "Father forgiven them for they know not what they do" As she read, "for they know not what they do", the words seemed to jump out at her and her heart softened. Tears came to her eyes as she realized that her friend really did not know how she had been hurt. This assurance from God brought the heart forgiveness and all the hurt and anger immediately went away and peace settled in.. She was able to share that with her doctor who was also encouraged because she decorated her walls in the hopes to help her hurting patients. It also brought glory to God.

How can we all apply this application personally and be set free by it? Often, the person who hurts us is either not a Christian or has backslidden from Christ. In either case, that person really does not know what he/she is doing. Oh, I know the person is probably aware of, and even wanting, to hurt with the offense, but he/she does not really know the extent of the pain it brings. Why? Because only the Holy Spirit can break our hearts and cause us to see the pain we have inflicted on someone. A non-Christian does not have the Holy Spirit inside. The backslidden Christian has grieved the Holy Spirit and He is not sensitive to the inner leading of the Spirit. The Holy Spirit is the ONLY Person who can penetrate that hardness of heart from either a Christian or a non-Christian. All we can do is forgive and realize that the person, if broken by the Holy Spirit, will see the pain he/she has caused. We can pray for that brokenness and offer God's grace which we ourselves need so badly. The Bible says that there is no righteousness in any of us, neither the one offended nor the one who offends, so we have to be careful not to be self-righteous in our judgment of someone who hurts us.

The ultimate purpose of God wanting us to forgive just as He forgives us is so that He may be glorified. When you agree to go beyond mental assent of forgiveness and bless the one who hurt you, the life of Jesus is revealed in you. And that is what brings glory to God. Colossians 3 vs. 12-13 sums it up pretty well.

Colossians 3 vs. 12-13

> *"Therefore, as God's chosen people, holy and dearly loved, clothe yourself with compassion, kindness, humility, gentleness and patience. Bear with each other and forgive whatever grievances you may have against one another. Forgive as the Lord forgave you."*

CHAPTER 9 -

"IF YOU LOVE ME", JESUS SAID

I got interested in reading about the last days that Jesus had with His disciples. In John, Chapter 12 vs. 19, John gives a detailed account of the last moments Jesus had with His disciples. One of the things that stuck out in my mind when I read this was when Jesus said, "If you love Me". There are only a couple of places in the Bible where Jesus actually said, "If you love me" — you will do something. I do not believe Jesus was necessarily putting any stipulations on love; however, He did say, "If you love me". In each case, He was referring to keeping His command or commandments.

John 14: vs. 15

"If you love me, you will obey what I command."

If you think about it, the act of love requires a response. How can you love or be loved without something happening. Love is a powerful bond between two people. In fact, it is *the* most powerful bond that exists between two people. The act

of love requires a response. “If you love Me, you will obey my commands”, Jesus said.
John 14: vs. 21

> *“Whoever has my commands and obeys them, he is the one who loves me. He who loves me will be loved by my Father, and I too will love him and show myself to him.”*

This is also a very interesting scripture. The part that is very interesting is where it says, “I too will love him and show myself to him”. The part that says, “show myself to him” is very intriguing. The scripture sometimes is a mystery to those who do not know Jesus. I don’t know if that relates to the fact that He does not show Himself to them or they do not have the ability to see things through Scriptural eyes. This is very interesting.

Keeping My Commandments

The next question that is of interest is, what are the commandments Jesus was referring to? The commandments are very clearly given in Mark 10: vs. 19.

Mark 10: vs. 19

> *“You know the commandments: ‘Do not murder, do not commit adultery, do not steal, do not give false testimony, do not defraud, honor your father and mother’.”*

If you go on to read the entire text of that commandment, you would need to read Mark 10: vs. 17-21. The same commandments appear in Matthew 19 vs. 16-21.

Mark 10: vs. 17-21

"As Jesus started on his way, a man ran up to him and fell on his knees before him. 'Good teacher,' he asked, 'what must a man do to inherit eternal life'? 'No one is good—except God alone. You know the commandments: 'Do not murder, do not commit adultery, do not steal, do not give false testimony, do not defraud, honor your father and mother.' 'Teacher," he declared, "all these I have kept since I was a boy'. Jesus looked at him and loved him. 'One thing you lack,' he said. 'Go, sell everything you have and give to the poor, and you will have a treasure in heaven. Then come, follow me'."

Matthew 19: vs. 16-21

"Now a man came up to Jesus and asked, 'Teacher, what good thing must I do to get eternal life?' 'Why do you ask me about what is good?' Jesus replied. 'There is only One who is good. If you want to enter life, obey the commandments.' 'Which ones?' the man inquired. Jesus replied. 'Do not murder, do not commit adultery, do not steal, do not give false testimony, honor your father and mother and love your neighbor as yourself'. 'All these I have kept', the young man said. 'What do I still lack?' Jesus answered, 'If you want to be perfect, go; sell your possessions and give to the poor, and you will have treasure in heaven. Then come follow me'."

Notice the perplexing response that Jesus gave the man when the man said, "I have kept the commandments". Jesus said, "Sell your possessions and give to the poor". Jesus was asking from this man the ultimate expression of love, giving what he valued most, and a complete commitment to His Father and to Him.

Probably the hardest of all the commands Jesus gave us while on this earth are found in Matthew 5 and Luke 6. What Jesus requires in these commands goes far beyond the submission necessary to feed the hungry, clothe the poor, visit the prisoners, etc. These commands require something that we do not have in our own strength—a willingness to suffer wrong without retaliating—the very thing that goes most against our human nature.

Matthew 5: vs. 38-41

> *"You have heard it said 'Eye for eye and tooth for tooth'. But I tell you, do not resist an evil person. If someone strikes you on the right cheek, turn to him the other also. And if someone wants to sue you and take your tunic, let him have your cloak as well. If someone forces you to go one mile, go with him two miles".*

Matthew 5: vs. 43-46

> *"You have heard that it was said, 'Love your neighbor and hate your enemy'. But I tell you to love your enemies. Bless them that curse you. Do good to them that hate you and pray for them who despitefully use you and persecute you; that you may be the children of your Father which is in heaven, for He makes the sun to rise on the evil and the good and sends rain on the righteous and the unrighteous. If you love those who love you, what reward will you get? Do not even the heathen do the same"?*

And in Luke, we read these words from Jesus:

> *"But I tell you who hear me: Love your enemies; do good to those who hate you. Bless those who curse you. Pray for those who mistreat you. If someone strikes you on one cheek, turn to him the other also. If someone takes your cloak, do not stop him from taking your tunic also.*
>
> *"If you love only those who love you, what credit is that to you? Even sinners love those who love them. And if you do good to those who do good to you, what credit is that to you? Even sinners do that. But, love your enemies; do good to them, and lend to them without expecting anything back. Then your reward will be great and you will be sons of the Most High, because He is kind to the ungrateful and wicked. Be merciful, just as your Father is merciful".*

These scriptures make it clear that God requires that we give to others the same mercy and grace that He shows to us in order to be called the "***children of your Father***", or the "***sons of the Most High***", and that is mercy and grace that is not earned or deserved.

Jesus also discussed another set of commandments when the Pharisees approached Him. The Pharisees asked a question that they thought would be the question that would trap Jesus, "which of the commandments is the greatest?" Jesus verified another set of commandments. Matthew 22: vs. 34-40.

Matthew 22: vs. 34-40

> *"Hearing that Jesus had silenced the Sadducees, the Pharisees got together. One of them, an expert*

in the law, tested Jesus with this question: 'Teacher, which is the greatest commandment in the Law'? Jesus replied: 'Love the Lord your God with all your heart and with all your soul and with all your mind.' This is the first and greatest commandment. And the second is like it: 'Love your neighbor as yourself.' All the Law and the Prophets hang on these two commandments."

As you can see by reading these scriptures, Jesus said if you were to obey the first two commandments, you have inasmuch as obeyed all of the rest.

The above commandments were given directly by Jesus. But, He also had some indirect commandments given to His people. One commandment given was The Great Commission found in the book of Matthew.

Matthew 28: vs. 16-20

"Then the eleven disciples went to Galilee, to the mountain where Jesus had told them to go. When they saw him, they worshipped him; but some doubted. Then Jesus came to them and said, "All authority in heaven and on earth has been given to me. Therefore go and make disciples of all nations, baptizing them in the name of the Father and of the Son and of the Holy Spirit, and teaching them to obey everything I have commanded you. And surely I will be with you always, to the very end of the age."

This commandment is referred to as The Great Commission. The Great Commission appoints us all as ambassadors of the New Covenant. God expects us to be His ambassadors; instead of conquering by war, He will conquer by love through His ambassadors.

The next indirect commandment demonstrated his passion and love for all of His people - even the people that were considered to be the least by the social standards of the day. Oh, how Jesus loved the least of the people by social standard.

Matthew 25: vs. 40

> *"When you've done this unto the least of these, you've done it unto Me".*

Jesus also gave another warning as a commandment. The one that, in my mind, sticks out to be the biggest warning deals with hypocrites and hypocrisy. In the book of Matthew alone, there are fifteen references to hypocrisy or hypocrites. In not one single case was Jesus speaking of hypocrisy as a noble and virtuous trait. As a matter of fact, if you were to read Matthew 24: vs. 51 you would see that Jesus assigns hypocrites to a place of weeping and gnashing of teeth.

Matthew 24: vs. 51

> *"He will cut him to pieces and assign him a place with the hypocrites, where there will be weeping and gnashing of teeth".*

Hypocrisy is the pretense of having possessions of feelings, characteristics or actions that one does not possess, especially, the deceitful assumption of praiseworthy qualities. Hypocrisy denotes a presumption of admirable qualities such as goodness, sincerity, and honesty by those who actually have the opposite qualities. Since they are unwilling to practice the very qualities that they aspire to, it becomes a practice of dishonesty and deceptiveness. It is a disguise of the real truth and heart of the person. In street talk it is simply said this way: You ain't what you say you are.

CONCLUSION

I have had a chance to look at the very elements and character and the nature of what Jesus was referring to when He said, "If you love me..." The depth of that expression of love will show itself by the way you keep His commandments. The next question that follows is this—What was the purpose of the commandments and why were they given?

The purpose of the commandments. If you study the commandments, you will see that each Commandment is designed to protect each and every person in God's creation. Each commandment was designed to protect each and every person in His creation. Each commandment is designed so that no person would hurt another person. He has given these commandments so that there can be total harmony among the people of His creation. In these particular commandments, He has made no reference to attending church services or Bible studies, although He does later, through Paul's writings. In these passages, Jesus made no references to building church buildings, or to any things of a works nature. Quite to the contrary, He is instructing people to go out into the world and to be His ambassadors and to show people how to give and forgive and preach the method of salvation. As I see it, that's what the great commandments are all about and we, the ambassadors, need to be on a mission to do what God has called us to do and in the way He has called us to do it. Abraham and Moses are dead. We are now the ambassadors. Hopefully, this is as meaningful to you as it has been for me.

PROMISES AND COMMANDS

"As the Father has loved me, so have I loved you. Now remain in my love. If you obey my commands, you will remain in my love, just as I have obeyed my Father's commands and remain in his love. I have told you this so that my joy may be in you and that your joy may be complete. My command is this: Love each other as I have loved you. Greater love has no one than this, that one lay down his life for his friends. You are my friends if you do what I command. I no longer call you servants, because a servant does not know his master's business. Instead, I have called you friends, for everything that I learned from my Father I have made known to you. You did not choose me, but I chose you to go and bear fruit - fruit that will last. Then the Father will give you whatever you ask in my name".

- John 15 vs.9-16

These verses are rich with the character and wisdom of our God. These verses give two important promises from God that we have heard of so many times that are used mostly out of context. With these promises, God also gives two very important commandments. Both of the promises are conditional.

THE PROMISES. The above verses speak of two promises. The promises are "Joy" and "The Father will give you whatever you ask in my name". Yes. These are promises, but they are conditional promises. The promises are conditional to obeying the Father's commands.

"Joy" - Read the following verses 10 and 11 from John 15:

> *"If you obey my commands, you will remain in my love, just as I have obeyed my Father's commands and remain in his love. I have told you this so that my joy may be in* ***you and that your joy may be complete."*** *(Bold type mine.)*

These verses say that you can have joy if you obey Christ's commands and remain in His love. After reading these verses, you have found the conditional secret to joy.

"The Father will give you whatever you ask in my name". Read the following verse 16:

> *"You did not choose me, but I chose you to go and bear fruit - fruit that will last. Then, the Father will give you whatever you ask in my name."*

Notice that this promise is also conditional. The promise is preceded by the word "then". The word "then" makes the promise contingent on obeying the commands, and it appears to include bearing fruit that will last. Another condition is that you ask "in my name".

This scripture, "The Father will give you whatever you ask in My name," can easily be used to justify a person's own vanity, which is self-serving ambition, or to gratify their own desires rather than God's plans for their life. As you will see, Jesus did not intend or desire this scripture to be used for self gain. The desire for this scripture is that we grow in righteousness and commitment to our calling. God wants to serve you in ways you can serve the intention of his creation.

Just to make a clarification of what it means "whatever you ask in my name" – it seems this scripture is easily, manipulatively and unwisely misused. The Greek meaning of the phrase "in my name" means to ask whatever is in line with Christ's character and will. Let me repeat that. **The Greek meaning of the phrase "in my name" means to ask what-**

ever is in line with Christ's character and God's will. A New Testament scripture supports the Greek meaning:

1 John 5 vs. 14

> *"This is the assurance we have in approaching God: that if we ask anything according to his will, he hears us."*

All the blessings and responses to prayers spoken of in the New Testament are contingent on God's people obeying His commands. The corporate body, the so-called church community, is also held to the standard of obeying the commands laid out by Jesus.

A REVELATION REVEALED

Silver and Hidden Treasure

Proverbs 2 vs. 1-6 says:

> *"My son, if you accept my words and store up my commands within you, turning your ear to wisdom and applying your heart to understanding, and if you look for it as for silver and search for it as for hidden treasure, then you will understand the fear of the Lord and find the knowledge of God. For the Lord gives wisdom and from his mouth come knowledge and understanding."*

Notice how God instructed His people to find the secrets of His wisdom and knowledge. Seek God's truths as though you were seeking silver and hidden treasure.

Jesus is revealing to us silver and a hidden treasure. Jesus sandwiches in a revelation between His promises and His commands. Read the following verses John 15:14-15:
"You are my friends if you do what I command. I no longer call you servants, because a servant does not know his master's business. Instead, I have called you friends, for everything that I learned from the Father I have made known to you."

I love it! Jesus is letting us know that we are fully prepared to know all there is to know about being His ambassadors. He said He has revealed to us all that the Father has revealed to Him. WOW!

Another revelation of silver and hidden treasure that coincides with what Jesus said shows up in Hebrews 8, vs. 7-13:

> *"For if there had been nothing wrong with that first covenant, no place would have been sought for another. But God found fault with the people and said: The time is coming, declares the Lord, when I will make a new covenant with the house of Israel and with the house of Judah. It will not be like the covenant I made with their forefathers when I took them by the hand to led them out of Egypt because they did not remain faithful to my covenant, and I turned away from them, declares the Lord. This is the covenant I will make with the house of Israel after that time, declares the Lord. I will put my laws in their minds and write them on their hearts. I will be their God, and they will be my people. No longer will a man teach his neighbor, or a man his brother, saying 'Know the Lord,' because they will all know me, from the least of them to the greatest. For I will forgive their wickedness and will remember their sins no more. By calling this covenant "new", he has*

made the first one obsolete, and what is obsolete and aging will soon disappear."

Notice that God said He put His laws in our minds and wrote them in our hearts. He goes on in the book of Hebrews to say that we are fully prepared and responsible to be His ambassadors.

Jesus is revealing one more piece of silver and hidden treasure in John 15 vs. 12-13:

"My command is this: Love each other as I have loved you. Greater love has no one than this, that one lay down his life for his friends."

These verses illustrate how our Holy Father used Jesus to transition from separation, as He did in the first covenant (because of man's sin), to a very personal and intimate relationship with man. He now calls man His friend and gives the reason for it. He also describes and defines His love for man when he said the greatest act of love from one man to another is when he lays down his life for that man. Jesus knew the rest of the story. He knew that the cross was out in front of Him and that He would have to demonstrate the greatest act of love by laying down His life for us.

CHAPTER 10 -

THE ISLAMIC RELIGION AND MUSLIMS

PREFACE

Out of a curiosity to know what is fact and what is fiction, I committed to study the belief system of Islam and its Muslim followers. Many sources of information were used in my study. I studied portions of the Koran, interpretations of the Koran, articles written by writers sympathetic to the Koran and writers critical of the Koran. I also studied information generated off the Internet. The following is a synopsis of my study and analysis. To keep this brief, I omitted most of the detail and tried to deal in concepts.

THE LIFE OF MUHAMMAD AND THE BIRTH OF THE KORAN

It was interesting to study the life and character of Muhammad. He was a very troubled man with a hard beginning. There are some accounts that, among other things, he was an epileptic. In the study of behavioral traits provided by the science of psychology, it is universally accepted that people of an epileptic background have an overpowering interest in the supernatural and the spiritual. That may be one of the primary forces that caused Muhammad to contemplate the perceptions of God. Also, probably because of his traumatic beginning, he appeared to be introspective and dealt with a self worth and identity problem. This may also have caused him to seek truth and a source of truth. A lack of identity and self worth may have caused him to ponder the reality of life. Much of his life was spent in seclusion in caves interpreting what he believed to be visions and prophetic truth from God.

Muhammad was believed to have been born in 570 A.D. He was born from the clan of Hasid, which was from the tribe of Quasash. His father died before he was born and his mother died when he was six. He was raised by one uncle and a nurse. In later years, he became a trader with a good reputation of honesty. His occupation as a trader took him to Syria where he mingled with Christians and Jews. It is believed that as he traveled to Mecca, he listened to Christians and Jews expound on their religious views. Because their views differed and there appeared to be conflicting absolutes, he was often troubled and perplexed. He withdrew to a cave outside of Mecca to sort out these differences, to meditate and to pray for guidance. During many of these meditations, he would appear to be in a seizure and would enter into a catatonic state. During this catatonic state, he would make utterances, which were later recorded as revelations from God. (History records similar occurrences in the New Testament. These people were not possessed of God, but possessed by demons from Satan. Perhaps this was Satan controlling Muhammad as well.) During one of his meditations, he had a vision that the archangel, Gabriel, came to him and declared him a prophet of God. His reaction was confounding and perplexing. He had many doubts concerning this vision. Even though he had doubts in the beginning, his wife convinced him that he was a prophet. (His wife was once his employer whom he eventually married.) His wife and cousin constantly reassured him of his status as a prophet. He spent much time in meditation in his cave and perceived many revelations, which were recorded. At his wife's encouragement, he began preaching publicly. These revelations became known as the Quran (Koran).

Muhammad began a movement that grew slowly but drew endorsement from some prominent people. Muhammad asserted himself as the last prophet of God and superseding all other prophets. He called for social reform that favored the poor, the slaves, the orphans, etc. In a sense, he became a "Robin Hood" who drew recruits and followers from the poor and uneducated. His mission also aroused enmity from the rich merchants. This was the beginning of division of the people of that area. That division later grew to the region and ultimately worldwide.

Muhammad's wife and uncle both died in 619 A.D. This was devastating to him and caused great despair and may also have induced a personality transformation. His mission became more aggressive over a five-year period. Through a strange turn of events, he was given supreme authority in Medina. With this authority, he enforced the ritual practice of Islam and mandated social reform based on his revelations that were known as the Koran. For the next years he became a warring leader and was a very shrewd military leader. He soundly defeated the Meccans and eventually massacred many Jewish men who opposed his Koran theology. After his military victories, the subjects were converted to the principles of Islam. He would conquer and convert; then conquer and convert. His method of conquering and converting may have been the catalyst that propelled the Islam religion in its infancy. To many, and maybe to most, he himself became the object of worship.

After his first wife died, he married and maintained a relationship with at least nine other women. Those women gave him many sons. All of his sons died in infancy. Only one daughter survived. Her name was Fatima.

Muhammad died of a sudden unknown cause on June 8, 632. After his death, most of his followers embellished the deity of his life through much mythology.

TERMINOLOGY & BELIEF SYSTEMS BY TOPIC

Outlined below are some interesting aspects of the belief system advocated by Muhammad through his Koran:

ALLAH

Allah is an Arabic word for "one god." Muhammad proposed that there is only one deified God and that is Allah. Because Christians believe in God the Father, God the Son and God the Holy Spirit, he labeled Christianity as a polytheistic religion. Muhammad is very clear on this as stated in the Koran in Sura 4:171, 5:72-73, and 4:169. Muslims cannot put it together that God the Father, God the Son, and God the Holy Spirit are one God in three persons.

ISLAM

Islam in its purest form means "peace and submission." Its theoretical meaning is "peace through submission to God." The underlying forces driving this theoretical position are the elements of submission. Does submission mean Jihad (committing murder under the name of "Holy War") or performing all of the various acts of ritualism to please Allah and earn a way into a higher place at death? The mandatory rule of submission is a very compelling and controlling force. The concept of submission is very dangerous when a man or group of men have the authority to determine the parameters of submission. As an example, an act of submission to Allah is to fly a passenger jet into a heavily populated building for the purpose of killing as many people as possible just for the sake of killing (9-11-01).

The rewards of submission are interesting. A Muslim man is led to believe that if he dies a martyr death (as happened on 9-11-01), he will go to a heaven and have forty virgin women at his beckoning. The Koran teachings seem so contradictory. It teaches peace by way of violence.

MUSLIM

Muslim means "to submit to the will of God." The Muslims believe that Muhammad was given the revelations of God's will. There are two primary sects of Muslims outside the borders of the United States. On the inside of the United States borders there are four sects. The two sects outside the United States borders are "Shia" and "Sunni." Both sects share most of the views of Muhammad. The sect that is strictly a follower of Muhammad is the Sunni. The Shia has incorporated some reformed views advocated by Ali — Muhammad's son-in-law. The Sunni live mostly in Iran. The Shia is central to the Iraq belief system. The Sunni is the Islamic belief system scattered throughout the rest of the Muslim world. It is interesting to note that several wars between Iran and Iraq (in which thousands upon thousands of lives have been lost) have been based on the differing issues in their Islam beliefs.

JESUS

How do the fundamental Muslims view Jesus? There are varying accounts, but it is interesting that most accounts consider Him to be a prophet. Muhammad believed Jesus was divinely inspired through the Immaculate Conception but denied His deity. Muslim teaching does not deny the history of Jesus. The Islam religion claims that He was able to perform miracles as a prophet. Muslims believe that the miracles were performed under the power of a prophet but not as the Son of God. Question? Where did those Muslims of Muhammad's day think that power came from? Where do Muslims today think that power came from? The power to perform miracles could only have come from one of two sources, God or Satan. Jesus used His power to do good for others. Satan does not do good, so the power given to Jesus must have come from God to perform these wonderful miracles.

There is another interesting point in their teaching concerning Jesus. They deny over 100 prophecies, given by the prophecies of God, before the birth of Jesus which were 100% accurate and which foretold Jesus as the awaited Messiah and deliverer. Muslims deny Jesus' claim to be the Son of God. Because they deny Jesus, they therefore deny the Holy Spirit. THIS IS PURE IGNORANCE ON THEIR PART. They say they believe in the same God as Christians and Jews believe in - the God of all creation - and they acknowledge the prophets and then deny all of the prophecies foretold by the prophets about the coming of Jesus as Messiah. Here is the part that is hard for me to understand: If they deny Jesus, then how can they justify a self-proclaimed prophet that has no prophetic history? Muhammad has no prophetic history.

Look at the lives of both Jesus and Muhammad. Muhammad failed in many things with his biggest failure being that he died and remained dead. Jesus died only to live again in total Glory. History records that Jesus walked again among the people after His crucifixion and death. Muhammad has returned to dust. Jesus has returned to Heaven. We Christians have a tremendous responsibility to educate the Muslim people. If they were given an educated choice, I believe they would choose to follow Jesus.

MUSLIMS AND THE HEREAFTER

Muslims believe that Allah set up a system of accountability. They believe there is a heaven and a hell with admission criteria for both places. The works that are done on earth fall into one of the two criteria as credits or debits. Also, their faithfulness to the rituals is part of the criteria. Once again, the dangers of this type of theology is in determining who defines which works are necessary and to what extent have enough works been done to satisfy the one who defines the works that are necessary for a positive credit. A wicked man can set up some pretty nasty standards for works criteria. We are seeing that being played out right now on a worldwide basis.

JIHAD

Jihad means "a striving in the cause of God." There are various aspects of Jihad, and the highest level of Jihad is to "stand up to a tyrant (an infidel) and to take arms in defense of Islam." The "defense" or type of defense is declared by the ruling power of religious leadership. Have you ever heard of the old saying "the best defense is a good offense?" Evidently, Muhammad must have had that in mind when he wrote the Koran. To paraphrase the Koran (Sura 5:51, 81, 9:4-5, and 74), it is right to kill the infidel, to make war with the unbelievers and to slay the idolaters. This is only a sampling of many writings in the Koran which justify selective murder.

Guess who is considered to be the primary fields? You've got it! The Jews and Christians. Remember that the authority of the ruling religious leadership of the moment defines the method of war. This is dangerous stuff. It is dangerous for this reason: when any religion (in this case, Islam) allows any man to have supreme power and authority to interpret God's Word and His will, eventually that man's will, desires, and ambitions will take control. A point in case is Osama Bin Laden and the Taliban.

Note: This is not something I have read from either the Orthodox or Reformed Koran. This is what I heard from a Muslim who was converted to Christianity. He was once in the higher order of the Muslim belief system. If this is true, it goes a long way to explain why there are so many suicide bombings. Jihad becomes a way to redeem a life that was not compliant to Muhammad's standards..

In the Islam religion, it is believed that each person has an angel on the right shoulder and an angel on the left shoulder. The angel on the right shoulder records all the good that he does during the day. That includes all his prayers and rituals etc. The angel on the left records all the bad things that he does during the day. At the end of his life he may or may not be able to go to the Promised Land. Allah will weigh all measures of works and make a call on his eternal destiny.

There is an exception to the disposition of his works. If he commits Jihad he automatically goes to the Promised Land, no matter how good or bad his life was. If this is true, I now understand why a Muslim would be willing to kill other people for the pure sake of killing those who do not believe as they do. This act of killing will assure him an eternal life in the promised land.

SHARIA

Sharia is the comprehensive Muslim law. The Koran (Quron) and the ruling authority of the religious leadership of the moment derive the law. It governs their moral basis, the basis of beliefs, thcir ritualistic procedures and even their aspects of daily living as well as collective living. This is justified as a protection mechanism.

Note: This is not the extent of the rituals, customs, and beliefs of Islam. There are many more.

THE INCEPTION OF ISLAM IN THE UNITED STATES

The very roots of the Islam religious system in the United States were founded in the northern states of the United

States, initially in Detroit, Michigan. The introduction was primarily among the Black American community. While in the southern states there were various levels of overt oppression and segregation, the north dealt a crueler and more demoralizing covert oppression and segregation. During the 1920's, there was a large migration of black people from the south to the north in the hopes for an improved lifestyle. Most of these people were relegated to segregated sections of the inner cities. And they still are today. Those sections of the cities are called ghettos. They were given the worst jobs and were the first to be displaced in economic slowdowns. They were also left to stand in long lines for hours for cheese and bread. The black people became very miserable and disgruntled. The covert oppression of the north was harder to deal with than the overt oppression in the south. They were desperately looking for alternatives. Colin Akridge wrote, "Instead of looking for a spiritual savior who would deliver them from their sins, they wanted a carnal savior who would save them from their misery and poverty." This set the stage for what happened next.

A man named Wallace Fard Muhammad came to Detroit selling silks and artifacts. Little is known of this man's history except he came from the Middle East. While his occupation was of little influence, his message was revolutionary to the black community. He brought the black people a message they needed to hear and wanted to hear. He preached freedom, justice, and equality to his members of the "lost tribe of Shabazz in North America." (Interesting that Shabazz was the name of Malcolm X's daughter.) He preached that the blacks had a past, present, and a future. The timing was perfect and within a couple of years, he recruited 8,000-10,000 followers. Among his recruits was a man named Elijah Poole who later changed his name to Elijah Muhammad. Elijah Muhammad took the leadership role of Wallace Fard Muhammad and recruited many more members. The membership consisted of the poor and uneducated.

Elijah recruited well for the Nation of Islam. Probably his most famous recruit was in 1947 when he recruited Malcolm X. (The history of Malcolm X is radical and would require a separate report.) After Malcolm X was released from prison, he and Elijah teamed up to lead The Nation of Islam. These two split when Malcolm X confirmed that Elijah fathered children from very close associates of Malcolm X. At that point, Malcolm X turned to an orthodox form of Islam. His interest in the orthodox version of Islam took him to extensive forages in Africa and the Middle East. He actually participated in the Islamic pilgrimage to Mecca. During the period that Malcolm X was studying the orthodox Islam, a new member was recruited and was an understudy of Malcolm X. His name is Lewis Farrakhan.

Later, after Malcolm X was assassinated, another split in the structure of this organization occurred and Lewis Farrakhan formed his version of Islam. Now there are four versions of The Nation of Islam. Probably the most recognized version is led by Lewis Farrakhan. Outlined below are his doctrinal beliefs:

DOCTRINAL BELIEFS OF LEWIS FARRAKHAN THE NATURE OF GOD

<u>God is not spirit, but a man.</u>

"God is a man and we just cannot make Him other than man lest we make Him an inferior one. A spirit is subject to us and not we to the spirit."

"Allah came to us from the Holy City of Mecca, Arabia, in 1930. He used the name Wallace D. Fard, often signing it W. D. Fard. He came alone."

<u>God is one of many gods. (Polytheism)</u>

"The Black man's gods, according to the history He (Allah) taught me, have all been the Wisest."
"Six thousand years ago, or to be more exact, 6,600 years ago, as Allah taught me, our nation gave birth to another god whose name was Yacub."

The Person of Christ
Christ was only a mortal man and a prophet, not God.
"He (Jesus) was nothing more than a prophet..."
"Making the Son and the Holy Ghost the equal with the Father is absolutely sinful."

Christ did not rise from the dead.
"He (Jesus) was nothing more than a prophet and he has gone back to the earth, never to return alive."
"We know what happened to him 2,000 years ago. He cannot come back from the grave. He is not in heaven."

The Bible
It is incomplete.
"The Bible is not all Holy, nor is it all the word of God."

It is a poison book..
"The Bible is now being called the Poison Book by God Himself and who can deny that it is not poison? It has poisoned the very hearts and minds of the so-called Negroes so much that they can't agree with each other."

"The Bible is the graveyard of my poor people (the so-called Negroes). The Bible charges all of its Great Prophets with evil; it makes God guilty of an act of adultery by charging Him with being the father of

Mary's baby (Jesus). Again, it charges Noah and Lot with drunkenness and Lot with getting children by his daughter. What a Poison Book."

If you read this ideology closely, you will see that Farrakhan is, by logic, placing himself above all humanity and every god. Reason with me for a second. If God is omniscient (knowing all things), then Farrakhan would also have to be omniscient and to a greater extent than God to know that God is not who He said He was. Farrakhan actually places himself above God. He is a very intelligent man with a tremendous power of persuasion. The question in my mind is this: Where does this power come from? It cannot come from God because his ideology disputes God. Lewis Farrakhan may be one of the most dangerous men on the earth today.

ISLAM'S MISSION IN THE U.S. TODAY

Islam's primary mission in the United States today is to be a refuge for the poor and uneducated black people. It is now also reaching out to the poor and uneducated white community as well. Islam still provides a sense of belonging and comradeship that gives its followers a sense of hope that someday they will rise above their impoverished circumstances. It is a false sense of hope but yet the only hope they see that they have. I would expect the Islam religion to grow at a very rapid rate in the years to come. Technology and education is polarizing wealth in the United States and, in fact, worldwide. The rich will become richer and the poor will remain poor. In fact, the rate of poverty will increase in the years to come. These higher poverty levels and less-educated levels will foster a climate for massive Islamic inbreeding. Islam and other belief systems like it will grow rapidly.

As I see it, the poor and uneducated black people are being victimized and they do not even know it. They have taken the bait and have fallen into the trap. People like Jesse Jackson keep preaching that there is a schism or an insurmountable separation between them and success. These people say that their color is against them or that the institution is against them or that the white people are against them or the law is against them. Jesse and others like him keep the people focused on the problem rather than the solution. This breeds a feeling of hopelessness. Jesse preaches that the only way to bridge this gap is through him, but he does not provide a way to bridge the gap. He preaches a welfare system that will keep them in their poverty. The Islam belief system comes in and says, "I have the way." One of the two major political systems does the same thing. Essentially, it says to the poor "You need me to protect you from the big, bad rich man and the mean institution." Without that ideology, that political system would have no platform. The other party says that the capitalistic system is tough. To do well, you must be smart and work hard. One party says "We will feed you" (which will keep you in poverty) and the other system says it will help you to rise to a level that you can learn to feed yourself. Which party do you think is which?

CONCLUSION

Satan is alive and well on planet earth today. He will use any means necessary to divert attention and reverence away from God the Father, His Son, Jesus, and the indwelling of the Holy Spirit. One of the most effective tools Satan uses for control is to set up a form of government under a religious system. The religious government works like this: A man, or men, assumes the authority to intercede and interpret on God's behalf. This can be dangerous because a selfishly ambitious man can easily make an interpretation to accomplish his own agenda. To protect against this kind of controlling power, God says to test all things to the

Scriptures. If anything does not line up with the Scriptures, beware; it is not from God. The reason why Satan uses a religion-based government is because as part of our creation, God put within each of us a need for Him. If a religion is structured in the form of a government, the men running the government of the religion can determine the parameters of the belief system, therefore, providing a means to meeting that need to please a God while ultimately serving the goals of the government. Man will fill that need with some form of a god. It is our responsibility to help others see that this emptiness for a divine relationship can only be filled by the one true God, and only that God. Christians have a big job to do to expand beyond our own self interests and evangelize the world before the cults do.

In my study of many commentaries, articles, portions of the Koran, interpretations of the Koran and various writings (some sympathetic to and some critical of the Koran), my conclusion is that the Islamic belief system is a mixture of good and evil theology. Much of the Koran is contradictory. It will state something in one sentence and then contradict it in the next. Muhammad must have realized the Koran's contradictory content and then tried to justify it by blaming the contradictions on God when he stated in the Koran (Sura 4:82): "Will they (the infidels) not ponder on the Koran? If it had not come from God, they could have surely found in it many contradictions."

Most of the Koran speaks of good works. It stresses taking care of the poor and the displaced. It is sympathetic to the poor and uneducated. In fact, Islam has an event called Zakat where the rich share their wealth with the poor. All of these things are good, but they are not the basis for a relationship with God the Father. Jesus is the only way to God the Father. Because Islam has a "good works" basis and because it offers a ray of hope through rituals and works, this belief system preys upon the poor and the uneducated. The Islam's field of prospects is limitless. The world is full of the poor and the uneducated.

The evil side of Islam is extremely clear. Muslims are not to befriend the infidels (Jews and Christians). In fact, they are instructed to kill and destroy the infidels (Sura 4:46-108). Example: In Sura 4:89 we read "They would have you disbelieve as they themselves have disbelieved so that you may be all alike. Do not befriend them until they have fled their homes in the cause of Allah. If they resist you, seize them and put them to death wherever you find them."

As I see it, individual Christians and the Christian church of today need to fight (in a figurative sense) for what is theirs and that is a lost and dying world which is being given over to Satan and his army. The Body of Christ is failing. Instead of building bigger churches, it should be building bigger areas of influence - evangelizing the world. It is not the unsaved person's fault if he/she has not heard the message of Jesus Christ; it is the fault of the Body of Christ. I, being a Christian, am at fault also.

PRAYER TIME, November 26, 2001

I HAD MY MORNING QUIET TIME, AND I WAS PRAYING AND ASKING THE LORD WHY THE MUSLIM, OR ISLAM, FAITH IS DOING SO WELL IN THE UNITED STATES. THESE THOUGHTS CAME TO ME. THEY MIGHT NOT BE GIVEN FROM THE LORD. HOWEVER, THEY JUST CAME AND I WANTED TO WRITE THEM DOWN.

QUESTION: HOW CAN THE MUSLIM, OR ISLAM, FAITH BE THE FASTEST GROWING RELIGION IN THE UNITED STATES AT THIS TIME? IN ADDITION TO THAT, HOW CAN

CHRISTIANITY BE ONE OF THE FASTEST GROWING RELIGIONS OUTSIDE OF THE UNITED STATES?

THOUGHTS THAT CAME TO ME:

Christians put a tremendous emphasis on their own church community (their church). Most of their energy and resources are given to develop their own church body, which often evolves into isolation, exclusiveness and then elevation. After elevation, history has shown, the church can evolve into extinction. Look at the once great churches of England and Europe which today are almost empty. Often times the Christian body (the church) operates independently of other church bodies, rather than collectively. This can cause the Christian body to be less effective and gives the impression of division and calamity. It often gives the impression that Jesus resides in certain cells or at least favors some of these individual cells, rather than the Jesus-based Christian body of believers. Another problem is this: These church bodies usually require membership. The membership often gives the connotation of social/economic or ethnic or physiological membership parameters and conditions. These membership conditions or parameters can be intimidating and emanate exclusiveness.

Why is the Muslim or Islam religion doing so well here in the United States? Because they present a unified message which gives them a great deal of unified power and control and a feeling of total unity. Also, it tends to dispel any social, economic, or ethnic barriers. Membership is not required and denominations within their faith do not exist. Their theme is universal and their focus is on membership by acceptance.

Why is the Christian outreach doing so well outside the United States? The reason may be for the same reason the Muslim, or Islam, faith is doing so well in the United States.

The Christians in the mission field have a more unified cause and they have no implication of social, economic, or ethnic barriers. Maybe the greatest advantage is in the fact that they are not inhibited in their work by trying to spend 90% of their energy and resources to develop a church cell. Their focus is mainly on winning souls and serving the Lord through the universal body of Christ.

CHAPTER 11 -

PLEA TO CHRISTIANS: WAKE UP AND SMELL THE MUSLIMS

PREFACE

The first paper I wrote on the Islam religion, entitled "The Islamic Religion and Muslims, was done to expose the evolution of the Islamic belief system and the incredible lunacy of the inception of the Koran. This chapter deals directly with the basic driving force behind the Islam religious system and how the Islam belief system can impact our culture and our way of life.

Recently, I completed an extensive study of the Islam religion to know for a fact what we as Christians are dealing with. My conclusion is disturbing and frightening. Stated very simply and very directly, the Islam religion is commissioned to kill the Jews and Christians. Following are some quotes from the Koran. As you read these, notice the repeated references and encouragement to fight. In some cases, they refer to fighting for the cause of God. It will help you in reading this to know that later on the Koran refers to one of the causes of God as being the elimination of the infidels, which causes me to question the character of their God. An infidel is anyone who does not believe in Allah, primarily a Jew or a Christian. Recently, we are hearing from the media and other sources that the Islam religion is not a violent religion. After reading the following passages from the Koran, which is Islam's bible, how can you draw any other conclusion than this is a violent religion?

Sura 4:86 – "They would have you disbelieve as they themselves disbelieved so that you may all be alike. Do not befriend them until they have fled their homes in the cause of God. If they desert you, seize them and put them to death."

Sura 4:91 – "Others you will find who seek security from you as well as from their own people. Whenever they are called back to sedition, they plunge into it headlong. If these do not keep their distance from you, if they neither offer you peace nor cease their hostilities against you, lay hold of them and kill them wherever you find them."

Sura 4:103 – "Seek out the enemy relentlessly. If you have suffered, they too have suffered; but you at least hope to receive from God what they cannot hope for."

Sura 8:12 – "God revealed His will to the angels, saying, 'I shall be with you. Give courage to the believers. I shall cast terror into the hearts of the infidels. Strike off their heads; strike off the very tips of their fingers.'"

Sura 8:19 – "Let not the unbelievers think that they will ever get away. They have not the power to do so. Muster against them all the men and cavalry at your commands, so that you may strike terror into the enemy of God and your enemy."

Sura 9:5 – "When the sacred months are over, slay the idolaters wherever you find them. Arrest them; besiege them and lie in ambush everywhere for them."

Sura 9:27 – "Fight against such of those to whom the Scriptures were given as believe in neither God nor the Last Day and who do not embrace the true faith until they are utterly subdued. The Jews say Ezra is the son of God, while the Christians say the Messiah is the son of God. Such are their assertions…how perverse they are!"

Sura 9:37-39 – "Believers, why is it that when you are told 'March in the cause of God, you linger slothfully in the land?' If you do not go to war, He will punish you sternly. Whether unarmed or well-equipped, march on and fight for the cause of God."

Islam has a program that is extremely calculated to achieve an end – eliminating the infidels. Example: The deliberate and calculated attack on September 11, 2001. That was an extremely well planned program to kill the innocent. Look also at all the other calculated attacks across the world with specific attention given to the destruction of Jews and Christians. Also consider the Palestinians' unprovoked attacks against Jews in Israel. The greatest potential attack on our culture (way of life) here in the United States and specifically to the Jews and Christians is not the obvious terrorist attacks of unmitigated terror and overt killings, but the calculated intentions and programs already in place to overthrow the U.S. government from within. There is a tremendous move by the Muslims within the United States to control this country. When the first Muslims came to this country in 1921, their stated intent was to overthrow the United States government. Their intent has not changed. The Muslims are infiltrating every form of our political system with the intent to rule over our system. One article that I read quoted from a former Muslim saying that Muslim men are marrying non-Muslims for the purpose of converting them to Islam and to merge the culture to make it difficult to segregate them for retaliation purposes. Now that is calculated.

Membership into the Muslim organizations is growing at an alarming rate in the United States and it is primarily in the black community with an increased movement in the uneducated, low income white community as well. They are very vocal about their intentions to overthrow our government. If you have any doubt about the mission of the Muslims in America, listen to Louis Farrakhan. He is the leader of the largest Muslim movement in the United States. The question is: Can the goals of the Muslim religion in America be successful? The answer is YES. Remember the holocaust? The Jews saw their demise coming but did nothing to alter it or prevent it. For the most part, they became lazy and self absorbed. They found a comfort zone and did not care what was going on around them. By the time they were forced to care, it was too late. I see the same thing going on in the United States. People in government and in the Christian church have become self absorbed, lazy and passive, and may have an attitude that says – if it is not affecting me personally, why should I care?

The Muslims are actively doing what the Christian community should be doing. They are engaged in offering hope through ministering to the poor and uneducated. This process allows them to propagate their ideals. They are the fastest growing religious organization in the United States today. The old adage still holds true – People do not care how much you know until they know how much you care.

WHAT CAN WE DO ABOUT THIS PROBLEM? This is a natural question and there are some answers. First of all, become aware of the issues involved and the potential consequences of those issues. Read for yourself the Koran and other sources of information to draw your own conclusions. Secondly, take action. As I talked to one gentleman about this situation, he said "What can I do? I cannot change the world." My response was this: "That may be right. You may not be able to change the world but you can change your world." Everyone has a sphere of influence. If you really want to do something, extend yourself inside your sphere. Go share what you know about your faith with your family, at your workplace, then your community, and ultimately do what Jesus commanded us to do – go into the world. A war will not solve this problem but a relationship will. Of course, a relationship with Jesus is the answer. So many Christians have become complacent, lazy and selfish, and self consumed. They are not doing what God has commanded us to do. He has commanded us to feed the hungry and help the poor. Too many of us have absorbed God's blessings and God's riches for our own pleasure and comfort. Christians need to get out and go about the business for which God put His people here.

In some ways, the organized church is also failing. Too many times a church is formed with good intentions. As time passes and God allows growth, they hoard His riches. They build bigger and bigger buildings and become more and more exclusive and self absorbed. Most even become territorial and discourage intermingling with other churches of like beliefs. This fragmentation is destroying our potential to unify our resources for the cause of God through Jesus Christ. We have to come together as a common body for the common cause of Jesus. Now, as to the bigger and bigger buildings I referred to: Of course we need a place of shelter and protection to "equip the saints for service" and I believe God would endorse that. But far too often the building becomes the object of the organization. If left to itself, that building will absorb most of the energy and resources of the organization.

Lastly, as I look upon the church body, I am reminded of an ancient Greek classic and can draw parallels. The Greek classic is The Last Days of Socrates by Plato. Socrates was put to death by the religious community of his day. Most people are led to believe that he was put to death because he was a non-believer. That is not true at all. He was put to death because he exposed the hypocrisy and piety of the religious people of that day. They professed to be religious and loyal to their religious teaching, but their lives did not reveal that teaching. Socrates did not dispute their religious belief. He simply observed the way they lived out their beliefs and saw a contradiction. Sometimes I wonder if Socrates were alive today, would he see the very same thing? If he exposed it, would the religious community react the same way? I know that history reports another person who exposed the religious community of their hypocrisy and piety and they crucified Him. Who do you think that person was?

OUTLINED BELOW ARE SOME OBSERVATIONS WORTHY OF THOUGHT:

The Proficiency of Jesus – Did Jesus know this Muslim organization would be established? Since he is all knowing, I think He did. He described their character and defined their creed when He gave this warning to us in John 16:1-3: "All this I have told you so that you will not go astray. They will put you out of the synagogue; in fact, a time is coming when anyone who kills you will think he is offering a service to God. They will do such things because they have not known the Father or me. I have told you this so that when the time comes you will remember that I warned you." The Muslims feel it is a service to Allah to kill the Jews and Christians.

Growth in Islamic Membership – Why is growth in the Islamic religion so rapid in the United States? Could it be that Muslims are doing what we Christians are commissioned to do? The Muslims are taking care of the homeless, feeding the poor and filling the spiritual need with their belief system. What is Jesus' commandment to His people in Matthew 25:31-46?

> *"When the Son of man comes in his glory and all the angels are with him, he will sit on his throne in heavenly glory. All the nations will be gathered before him, and he will separate the people one from another as*

a shepherd separates the sheep from the goats. He will put the sheep on his right and the goats on his left. Then the King will say to those on his right,' Come, you who are blessed by the Father; take your inheritance, the kingdom prepared for you since the creation of the world. For I was hungry and you gave me something to eat; I was thirsty and you gave me something to drink; I was a stranger and you invited me in. I needed clothes and you clothed me. I was sick and you looked after me; I was in prison and you came to visit me.' They also will answer, 'Lord, when did we see you hungry and feed you, or thirsty and give you something to drink? When did we see you a stranger and invite you in or needing clothes and clothe you? When did we see you sick or in prison and go to visit you? The King will reply, 'I tell you the truth. Whatever you did for one of the least of these brothers of mine you did for me.' Then he will say to those on his left: 'Depart from me, you who are cursed, into the eternal fire prepared for the devil and his angels. For I was hungry and you gave me nothing to eat. I was thirsty and you gave me nothing to drink. I was a stranger and you did not invite me in. I needed clothes and you did not clothe me. I was sick and in prison and you did not look after me.' They also will answer, 'Lord, when did we see you hungry or thirsty, or a stranger or needing clothes or sick or in prison and did not help you?' He will reply, 'I tell the truth. Whatever you did not do for one of the least of these, you did not do for me.' Then they will go away to eternal punishment, but the righteous to eternal life."

Question: Are God's warriors, we Christians, carrying out this mission or are Satan's warriors doing it? The Muslims (also the Mormons and all other cultic "isms") are winning in the membership battle by implementing these principles found in Matthew 25.

CHAPTER 12 -

MISCELLANEOUS THOUGHTS

THE MOUTH

The mouth—what a wonderful and important thing it can be. It allows you to enjoy some of the blessings of Our Lord. Some of the most joyful times are when we are using our mouths to eat. The mouth can also be a vital tool used to express and communicate through verbalization. The mouth, while it can be a nice thing, can also be a vicious tool or a weapon that can be used for pure destruction. More wars, destruction, and hurt has been brought about by words that come from the mouth, than any other mechanism.

Words can be a tool of destruction, but, words can also be a thing of beauty. What better mechanism for communication do we have than words coming from the mouth. Also, what feels better than a kind word that comes from the mouth?

The Bible has hundreds of references to the mouth in both the New and the Old Testament. The Bible records many cases where the mouth was a tool or a weapon. The Bible also records many cases in which the mouth gave words of comfort and joy and reassurances. In the New Testament, Jesus gave a statement about words used in the wrong way, Matthew 15:10. The mouth in this scripture is referred to as a weapon because of the words that come out of it. Refer to Matthew 15 vs.10-20. Verse 10 says it very clearly:

Matthew 15 vs.10

> *"Jesus called the crowd to Him and said, "Listen and understand. What goes into a man's mouth does not make him 'unclean', but what comes out of his mouth, that is what makes him 'unclean'."*

The rest of those verses, verses 10-20, go on to clarify what He is referring to – words. We all use them. Jesus said to be careful that your words are cleansing and be sure your words are clean, not unclean. This whole distortion is about this: the essence, character, and soul of a man is not so much about what a man puts into his body from the outside in, but rather the essence, character and soul of a man is reflected by what comes from the inside out through his words, deeds, and actions.

There are other warnings given in the Bible about the dangers of the mouth and tongue, and
how to use our tongues to build-up others.

Psalm 141 vs. 3

> *"Put a guard over my mouth, O Lord. Keep watch over the door of my lips."*

Psalm 39 vs. 1

> *"I said, 'I will guard my ways lest I sin with my tongue. I will restrain my mouth with a muzzle'."*

Psalm 19 vs. 14

> *"Let the words of my mouth and the meditation of my heart be acceptable in Your sight, O, Lord, my Strength and my Redeemer."*

Psalm 15 vs. 1

> *"A soft answer turns away wrath, but a harsh word stirs up anger."*

Proverbs 17 vs. 1

> *"The beginning of strife is like releasing water. Therefore, stop contention before a quarrel starts."*

James 1vs. 19

> *"Be quick to listen, slow to speak, and slow to become angry."*

Ephesians 4 vs. 29

> *"Do not let any unwholesome talk come out of your mouths, but only what is helpful for building others up according to their needs, that it may benefit those who listen."*

ATTITUDE/GRATITUDE

Gratitude is an attitude. Without an attitude of gratitude, then gratitude cannot be an attitude. It is the attitude of gratitude that minimizes the need for favorable circumstances in life for you to find joy and contentment. Without an attitude of gratitude, the price tag of joy and peace and contentment increases without an end. I am convinced that the impact of the circumstances of our life is 90% perception of those circumstances and 90% of those perceptions start with an attitude – an Attitude of Gratitude

.

I Timothy 6 vs. 6

"Godliness with contentment is great gain."

In this scripture, Paul does not say "Godliness with money" or "Godliness with a big house" or "Godliness with perfect relationships" or "Godliness with good health". It says "Godliness with contentment". What is contentment? The Greek word used in this scripture is *autarkeia"* which means "satisfaction with what one has". Contentment begins with an attitude – being thankful for what we have, not wishing for what we don't have – An Attitude of Gratitude!

EMOTIONALLY INVOLVED

It is easy to become emotionally involved in a circumstance or set of circumstances. Our decisions, based on emotions are often very bad decisions.

It would be wise to step back, wait for a little bit, think through what is going on and ask yourself, "What would the Lord do?"

At that point, you would be capable of making a good decision.

WHAT MAKES A WINNER?

Man O'War was the greatest race horse that ever lived. In his lifetime he ran only 21 races with a total racing time of 33 minutes, 32 seconds. Think about that. In all his life, Man

O'War ran in competition for only one-half hour. And that is what history remembers — only his races in competition.

But the days and weeks and months of stubborn and relentless training, the days and weeks and months with no one in the grandstands, with no one to cheer him on but his own desire and ambition — these were the important things. These were the things that really made him a champion. You see, he was good when he didn't have to be; he was good when no one else was watching. And that, to me, is the true mark of a champion.

Living a Christian life is certainly not like running a horse race; however, some of the principles can be generalized. The toughest, the most grueling competition in life is that which a Godly person sets up for himself when no one is watching. It's doing the job that our Lord wants done and doing it better than it need be done. It's the hours of unnoticed meditation, prayer, and study of His Word. It's that loneliness of a separated life. It's the unrewarded compassion and help offered to the less fortunate. It's simply being Godly when no one else thinks you have to be.

As for the victory — the world may see you as a loser, but the Lord will see a true thoroughbred. The Lord and the angels in heaven will declare you a champion for eternity!

SUCCESS/FAILURE

Failure is most often not in the results of a plan to succeed. Failure is the result of not having a plan to succeed. If the results of a plan to succeed did not turn out as expected, there is still success in that you have learned something.

GOOD/BAD

What does "good" mean? What does "bad" mean? You have heard the terms and spoken them frequently without much thought as to what they really mean. Example: I had a good/bad day, or, that person is a good/bad person. "Bad" is a term that in itself does not have a precise meaning and is without a dimension. That sounds strange, but it isn't. The term "bad" does not have a quantity or quality unless it is indexed to, or compared to, something that is more desirable than what it is compared to. As an example, you may think a flat tire on your car was bad until you compare it to a car wreck. Another example – You may think 90-degree weather is bad until you compare it to 105-degree weather. The 90-degree weather would, on a comparative basis, seem good. One more example – You may think stale bread is bad, but compare that to no bread at all or only moldy bread to eat, then stale bread becomes good. What is bad in one set of circumstances becomes good in another. Stale bread would be good to most people of the world since they have no bread, fresh or stale. Moral of the point of things that are considered bad: Bad is a measurement of varying levels of good. All things have some properties of "good" and they are only "bad" when compared to other things. Look for the good in all things, and you just may find the good and, therefore, be happy.

DIRECT MY PATH

If you are asking God to direct your path, you must be moving. If you are not moving, how can God change your direction? A person who is not moving has no direction, and, therefore, does not have a basis for change to start a new direction. Keep moving toward what you know as God's righteousness and will for you, and he will move you, direct your path and charter your course to fulfill the calling of your creation. Only than will you find total joy, peace and contentment. This is how, I believe, the martyrs were able to willingly give their lives for the namesake of our Lord Jesus.

The following scripture is good example of the importance of moving so that God can direct your path:

Isaiah 30 vs. 21

> *"Whenever you turn to the right or to the left, your ears will hear a voice behind you, saying, 'This is the way; walk in it'." NKJV*

This scripture seems to indicate that when we are trusting God to lead us, we can confidently move ahead, trusting Him to direct us in our way when we get off the path.

CHAPTER 13 -

INSPIRATIONAL THOUGHTS ON WHAT REALLY MATTERS - GOD'S OPINION OF YOU AND HIS PURPOSE FOR YOU

As part of my business practice, I send out annual birthday letters to each of my clients. These letters are prayerfully thought out and written, and deal mainly with the importance of their creation by God for His purpose. Over the years I have been told by so many clients how these letters have benefited them in their understanding of just how important their creation and day of birth is to God. I want to share excerpts from some of these letters with you, my readers, in the hope that you also will see just how important your creation was and how much God, the Father loves **you**!

It's Birthday Time

Isn't it wonderful to be living in these times here in the United States? It is truly a gift and a blessing from the Lord. Because of this gift, we have the freedom to openly, without fear of reprisal, take a day to celebrate a very important and special event. IT'S YOUR DAY OF BIRTH! Wow, what a wonderful day! I truly believe when the Lord created you, He celebrated. He created you to be significant, purposeful and by design to find fulfillment, happiness and joy in Him and in His sovereign plan for your life. You are important to Him. Your creation was the beginning of it all! May God bless you!

Shakespeare Was Partly Right

Shakespeare was known to say, "To be or not to be is the question". The pondering portion of this question is centered around the proposition of what does it mean "to be". As it relates to your birthday, "to be" is the question. By virtue of your "birth" day, you are no longer a "to be", but "you are". "You are" because Jesus said so! "You are" because you are His creation according to His purpose. Yes, "you are" is significant. "You are" His joy and delight. "You are" intended to find joy and peace according to His purpose. 'You are" a gift to all of mankind.

The Dash on Your Tombstone

"What is that dash for, Daddy"? the little boy said as they observed a grave stone in a cemetery. "Son, see that first date? That was when that person was born. And the other date over there – that is when that person died". "Okay, Daddy. But what is the dash for"? "Son, that dash between the two dates represents that person's life story. It represents all the good and bad things that were done and not done in the time between the date he was born and the date he died". "Daddy, will I have a dash?" "Son, you are building your own personal dash right now. God gave you a very special appointed day of birth – your birthday. Your special day of birth began the process, and God created you for a very important purpose so that your dash would represent an asset to Him and to mankind."

This conversation between father and son is also about you and your Creator Father. Your Heavenly Father wants you to know His purpose for you because He knows that fulfilling your purpose will give you joy and peace. He wants you to live in such a way that your dash will honor Him. It all began with a special day of creation – Your birthday! Have a wonderful "creation day" and build a beautiful "dash"!

Congratulations on Your Special Day!

It is your birthday! Most say it is just another day, but oh what a mistake! It is a **very special** day!! In fact, it is the most special day of your life, because it marks the beginning of your life. The Scriptures tell us that you are a creation – a very **special** creation, a creation with **special meaning**. Your joy, peace and fulfillment come with your pursuit of the purpose of your creation according to the master plan. Yes, there is a master plan, and part of that master plan comes back to birthdays. Your birthday is a **very special day**! It is a creation from God. How can anything be more special than that? Always remember that you are special and that God loves you!

Cause for Celebration

Is it enough to say Happy Birthday on such a special day? Would it be enough to sing Halleluiah on such a special day? Is it possible to make time stand still just to savor this special day a little longer? Take a minute and realize how special this day really is! God created the universe day by day by speaking it into existence. But, when it came to you (you special one), He hand made you and formed you into a likeness of Himself.

He did that so you could have meaning, significance and a designed purpose. Is it appropriate to say Happy Birthday and Halleluiah on this special day? Yes, and much more. You are a special, hand-designed gift to mankind!

Power to Choose

Power-Birthday, Power-Birthday, Power-Birthday. What is the connection? Is there a connection? Yes, there is a connection between Power and your Birthday. When you were born, which is your Birthday, you were granted Power. God gave you the Power to make choices. You have the Power to choose right from wrong – good from bad – to choose God's righteousness or not to choose God's righteousness – to choose to follow Christ or not to follow Christ. Making the right choices is vital because there will be a day when that Power will be taken away. You will stand before the Lord and either be glorified or terrified by the use of that Power given to you on your Birthday. Power-Birthday. Yes, there is a connection. Use your Power wisely. God loves you.

Your Birth Day Is Significant

Birthday. It is easy to say, but is it significant to say? Is it just another day? Does it have value? Okay, what is a birthday all about and what is its value? When God finished creating the universe and the earth, He considered it incomplete. Think about that. All that there is in the universe and earth was considered incomplete until God created man. And He considered it incomplete until He created you! Your birthday is special. It establishes that you are a special creation. God thinks you are special and your birthday is special. God values you and your birthday above all of His creation. Your part of His creation started on your "birth" day. Remember how valued you are. God created you and called you to be a special purpose.

As you end the reading of this book, remember: What really matters is that you know how special you are to God and that you find your purpose for life through the redemption He offers through His Son, Jesus Christ.

CPSIA information can be obtained at www.ICGtesting.com
Printed in the USA
LVOW12s2330251113

362766LV00002B/3/A

9 781600 345258